GLADSONG
AND
GATHERING

GLADSONGS AND GATHERINGS

Poetry and its social context in Liverpool since the 1960s

Edited by Stephen Wade

LIVERPOOL UNIVERSITY PRESS

First published 2001 by
Liverpool University Press
4 Cambridge Street
Liverpool L69 7ZU

British Library Cataloguing-in-Publication data
A British Library CIP record is available

ISBN 0-85323-727-1

Typeset by Northern Phototypesetting Co. Ltd, Bolton
Printed and bound in the European Union by Bell and Bain Ltd, Glasgow

I will make all that is possible step out of time
to a land of giant hoorays!

Brian Patten, *January Gladsong*

He Painted Poems...

He painted poems of an imaginary England
which was also the real one.
Something nasty beyond the shrubbery.
Eleven Dennis Nilsens disguised as Bruce Wayne
quietly eating their Campbell's soup
before opening that dark door Night.

But there is something real beyond the neon,
something he looked for in the ordinary
streets, in the kitchens and bedrooms,
with the ordinary names of lovers and heroes,
the names themselves their magic signs.

Roads and skyways the rolling backdrops
in between, he travelled ever hopefully
along the sweaty entangled valleys of love,
sending out detailed reports on the botany.

He liked to fold things in unusual ways
to see if they would jump or fly:
paper that flowered into banners of panties
like doves over city landscapes
where ghosts and the living mingle.

He planted imaginary gardens
full of real plastic daffodils
for the silent grandmothers
and the children who come after.

David Bateman

Contents

Acknowledgement

Peter Barry's essay, '"The Hard Lyric": Re-registering Liverpool Poetry', first appeared in *The Cambridge Quarterly* 28 (4), 1999, pp. 328–48. The editor is grateful to Oxford University Press for kindly giving permission for its inclusion in this volume.

Introduction

Stephen Wade

This book was prompted by a vague feeling that the city of Liverpool and the three poets associated with the now-celebrated *Mersey Sound* volume (in the Penguin Modern Poets series, 1967) presented an assortment of paradoxes. First, there was the notion that Liverpool was hardly a 'cultural centre' in the way that such a thing had been explained to me during my schooling. My secondary modern education in Leeds had led me to classify poetry as something that bore no relation to the pop lyrics of the late 1950s and early 1960s; yet critics were talking about Liverpool as a place of renaissance and music revolution.

Secondly, there was the realisation that the poets in that volume were somehow not the same as the poets I was given to study in the first year of my English degree. My friends and I separated Roger McGough from Stephen Spender but were unable to say why we did so. With hindsight, it is possible to see McGough, Adrian Henri and Brian Patten and their associated world of students, workers and musicians as a key element in a movement of literary renewal – one that was not conscious of being 'literary' at all.

Gladsongs and Gatherings, then, began with a conviction that McGough, Patten and Henri were important in British literary history for several reasons. Their attitudes, despite having literary antecedents in writers such as Arthur Rimbaud (1854–91), Allen Ginsberg (1926–97) and Adrian Mitchell (born 1932), were hard to define in performance, and it was surely the delivery and realisation of often throwaway lines that emphasised their achievement. Those who saw the performances in coffee bars and pubs attest to something different, a direct and somehow natural sensibility and wit that was already well established in the city and its people.

In the course of interviewing McGough and Patten in preparation for this collection, I became aware that the actual practitioners are reluctant to provide an explanation of what they did 30 years ago; in fact, their poetics is based largely on a specifically Romantic conviction that the self is not only central to creativity but generative of a dramatised instant of feeling. A McGough reading, for instance, often relies on the momentary insight of the *flaneur* (or 'idler'), as if the lyric is a celebration of the poetic attitude of standing back and taking time, rather than planning an agenda and writing poems to match.

For these reasons, as the planning of the book progressed, it became obvious that it would be pointless to wrap these reflections and critical essays in the vocabulary of modern literary or cultural theory. Everything written by these poets is antipathetic to the concerns of theory. Brian Patten, for instance, has little time for anything that aims to explain something that is essentially valuable only for its subjective insight. His definition of poetry concerns 'what you thought you had forgotten'; that is, words assembled in form and rhythm are integral to the self and its locus. Liverpool is the locus here.

The discussions in the essays and recollections gathered here offer some help in answering the persistent questions about the social context of poetry in Liverpool, but they also concern the issues raised in writing about a metropolis in a postmodern context. A critic may also legitimately ask about the other poets of the city, and what the legacy of the movement called 'the Mersey Sound' has been. It is clear from the memoirs collected here that the art is thriving. At a recent meeting of Carole Baldock's 'Dead Good Poets' Society' in the Everyman Bistro, it was obvious not only that the spirit of Mersey Sound's convivial company and tolerance had survived, but that writers had travelled considerable distances to be there. One poet from North Wales reminded outsiders that there is a strong bond between the Welsh and the Liverpudlians in their adherence to the poetic art. Overall, the performers at the gathering were impressively eclectic and exuberant.

There are also more fundamentally important questions to be asked here. The issue of metropolitan versus regional consciousness emerges, as it did for Edward Lucie-Smith in his book *The Liverpool Scene* (1967), discussed below. In this respect Liverpool has certain strikingly significant features. The central example is the sense of distance and isolation that is commonly felt there, and indeed was expressed by McGough in a recent essay:

> The thing about Liverpudlians is that we live in a city that looks out to the sea, and we feel cut off by land. If you take the East Lancs road out towards

Manchester, it is not long before 'our tribe' quite suddenly ends. There is no transition. The accent, loyalties, the sense of belonging stop abruptly.[1]

This is a feature of English regional awareness that was well established in Victorian writing – for example, the provincial urban pride of the Yorkshire and Lancashire industrial towns. It may be that there is an interesting link between the dialect writing of their almanacs and anthologies and the small magazines of the Liverpool clubs in the 1960s; but McGough's point is one of location and distance. The myth of the 'Scouser' in popular culture supports this; even in guidebooks to the city, the local wit and sense of identity is emphasised. Howard Channon, for example, pinpoints this quality:

Rob Wilton, Tommy Handley, Arthur Askey, Ted Ray, Ken Dodd and Jimmy Tarbuck are six names from generations of famous funny men who were cradled in a city where, for as long as anyone can remember, it has been claimed with a perverse pride that 'you have to be a ruddy comedian to stick the place.'[2]

Channon here discusses the popular representation of a comedic persona, often expressed almost as a stereotype of itself; but it is, nevertheless, easy to see this love of paradox, pun and allusion in the Mersey Sound poets. A cursory reading of the poems in the 1969 volume provides a sharp reminder of the elements of setting, local identity and projection of feeling which all sustain the stand-up comedian as well as the poet. Patten's early work was a creative mix of the French Symbolist desire to shock, childhood vocabulary and unashamedly unchecked emotive response, but the focal power was always comedic, playful and whimsical, affirming the function of poetry as entertainment by communal sharing and recognition of a universal condition tempered by a 'local habitation and a name'.

More recent images of the city have been mixed and confused. Visiting writers are perplexed by the explanations given of its unique qualities. The Russian journalist Vitaly Vitaliev went to Liverpool in June 1999 and was persuaded that the Blitz and the Victorian architecture presented some kind of explanation between them, but he concentrated on the over-familiar landscape that is certainly not what most Liverpudlian poets write about: 'Baedeker would have been horrified by the metropolitan Cathedral of Christ the King, known locally as "Paddy's Wigwam"...'[3] What Vitaliev did not mention was the persistence of the bohemian, freewheeling artistic sensibility in Liverpool, and the kind of constructive leisure that is exemplified in the new Concert Square with its cafes, galleries and DJ gatherings. The readers of poetry perhaps still want to see only the Liverpool represented by the black and white documentary photography which defined the arrival of Patten; images of smoke-filled pubs or a street full of litter, as published in his book *Little Johnny's Confession* (1967).

Spencer Leigh identifies something far more vibrant and meaningful in his account 'All You Need Is Words' (page 143), and he has reminded readers of the tendency for all performance artists to invent and reinvent their public personae. In his obituary of the lead singer of the Fourmost, Leigh notes that the Beatles had a 'domino effect' on attitudes to creativity, but he also stresses the locale and the identified audience: 'in 1962 they came 10th in a poll of local groups in *Mersey Beat*, no bad feat considering the competition...'[4]

The audience also had a real significance for the Mersey poets. As with the Beatles and the small groups playing in the clubs, it was the knowledge of the audience that changed attitudes. For example, Brian Epstein's talent-spotting in the city related to the sense of local identity he observed in his record shop. It was only his discovery of the magazine *Mersey Beat* and German imports of locally popular records that opened his eyes to the potency of the city and its aesthetics.

What brings all this together is the notion of a 'known' audience as part of the subject matter of the writing. McGough and Patten have said that they did not necessarily have working-class or student listeners in mind when they wrote, but their early work presents an enlightening example of poetry written almost by instinct for a recognisable audience, and – even more interesting – poetry with an emphasis on intonation and delivery rather than on substance. In McGough's case, he had become aware of this gap in the market when a student at Hull. His poems were rejected by the 'serious' literary magazines at first, and his recognition of what kind of work he was producing came from an awareness of the importance of his intonation and delivery. This is apparent in his total confidence, expressed in an interview in 1998, that he had never considered 're-inventing himself' as a performer since that first step towards success on the local cafe scene.

Lucie-Smith and *The Liverpool Scene*

There is no doubt that *The Liverpool Scene*, edited by Edward Lucie-Smith

(1967), has been seminal in its influence on the contemporary evaluation of the Liverpool writing. It openly gives context to the three poets, presenting them as manifestations of a vague Liverpool consciousness: 'But the city continues to think of itself as something pretty special', says Lucie-Smith, in the course of explaining the phenomenon.[5] The basis of his argument is that the lack of cultural hierarchies goes some way towards explaining the uniqueness of the city. 'A man trying to write poetry in Liverpool usually has the attitudes of a frontiersman', he says,[6] and the soundbites and photographs proceed to struggle to explain what is, from his London standpoint, a stunning paradox: How can an avant-garde movement be regional? Is it simply a fad? The photographic images contained in the book suggest bizarre paradoxes of French boulevardiers and intellectual/artistic indifference among the clutter of the mundane and the crassly banal. A typical image shows Henri, bearded and bespectacled, staring at the lens from the centre of a line of towering soup tins. The labels above a supermarket aisle border the top line of the frame. In a similarly surreal clash of connotations, later in the book we have Henri dressed as Alfred Jarry's Père Ubu, standing erect in a tree-fringed open field, an anorak over his stern expression.

Encapsulating this odd mix of images, and purposely juxtaposing the working class/regional and the metropolitan/bohemian/Modernist carelessness with any set agenda, is the photo of a street sign in Hope Street that has been embellished with graffiti saying 'Lenny is fat' and 'Liverpool are great'. What conclusions are we to draw here? One might explain the creative centre of Liverpool at this time as being formed by a lack of contact with any mainstream ideologies or established modes of artistic faith. The basis of the new working-class creativity is explained as raw, iconoclastic and without any intellectual encumbrances from the schoolroom or the seminar. As Henri says in an autobiographical piece (with reference to Bootle), 'Once you got out of school there was nothing. They lived on this estate and there was literally nothing but houses and three shops and a big wilderness in the middle and nothing else.'[7]

Lucie-Smith extends his enquiry to what all this says about the relation of entertainment to art, and raises the thorny subject of 'standards' of poetic craft in the writing. He is coping with the critical dilemma of trying to classify a movement that resists a taxonomy. In interviews as recent as 1998 and 1999, McGough and Patten have been reluctant to explain what lay behind the Lucie-Smith essay. In one sense, they are quite right to assert that the movement was spontaneous, driven by a desire to have fun and, above all, was generated by something indefinable in the Liverpool setting in the late 1960s. It was a galvanisation, perhaps, of a latent talent for expressing joy and celebration, and of the fragility of life in these open wastelands at what Larkin called, speaking of his forbidding Humberside dockland, 'the end of England'.

Interest from the United States in this complex fusion of imaginative interplay added to the intrigue. Certainly American influences are apparent, as Richard Stakes's essay in this book makes clear for the pop setting; it is also true of the poets and musicians. Pete Brown and jazz, Ginsberg and poetry, and Jack Kerouac (1922–69) and his myth of escape and lyrical fugitive freedom, were all influential figures. It has to do with a view of art as immediate, related to the street-song of the maimed veteran mentioned by Patten in the interview published here (see p. 103). It is also a part of the Liverpool of folk songs, a focus for immigration, cheap labour and working-class consciousness. The singing, the drinking, the jokes, the football – and the poetry.

For these reasons, Liverpool presents a case study in proletarian writing, perhaps more clearly than in the 1930s, when definitions were cluttered and confused by the urgent pressure to present a crusade for 'the masses' – whoever they are. Much of this proletarian sense is a continuation of the street literature of ballads, the oral tradition and that 'primary orality' discussed by Walter J. Ong in his account of communities in which writing is little used.[8] In short, Liverpool contained an audience for poetry which had no significant preconceptions about poetry when performed or simply read aloud.

Liverpool's history reinforced the importance of this proletarian writing; the Celtic and American elements, combined with native seafaring narratives and the inner-suburban toughness of life, contributed to the subject matter that would preoccupy the emerging poets.

The Small Magazines

Case studies of poetry and community, such as this one, often uncover a proliferation of small magazines produced by students or coteries, which illustrates the process by which attacks on moribund language and a sense of innovation in poetry tends to occur. Certainly Patten's desire to make his writing an existential statement as well as a social commentary illustrate this. In Liverpool the magazines had a notable impact on poetry in general, particularly surprising given that Liverpool was a place with no literary foundations or conventions of any real substance. In this it was no different from Leeds or Lincoln or Stoke, and the progress from small magazines to London-published collections is a remarkable cultural phenomenon.

Patten's *Underdog* was not the only small magazine. There was also *Contrasts*, edited by Russell Pemberton and John Dearing, as well as publications by Brian Wake's Driftwood company. *Underdog* illustrates the virtues of text-only publishing, and the names in Issue 8, for instance, show the magnitude of its achievement in attracting poets from both sides of the Atlantic: Mitchell, Ginsberg, Hollo, Horovitz and Milton appear alongside the local writers.

In some ways, though, *Contrasts* marks the period in a different way. It contained work by well-known names such as Pudney, Nuttall and Bold, but the underlying ideology was one of eclecticism and open-minded exploration. It actually appealed to readers in one issue with the words: 'Are you waiting to be discovered?' There is a sense of being involved in a daring enterprise in both magazines and, more significantly, they were looking towards Europe and North America. The local lies beside the cosmopolitan, and the evolution of a city's literary identity can be detected, alongside a sense of imminent achievement.

As with all small magazines, the focus was on experimentation. The pages allowed for working drafts; established writers appeared alongside new writers; and there was a feeling of literature being taken seriously, without descending into arrogance.

John Cornelius and *Liverpool 8*

In 1982 John Cornelius's book *Liverpool 8* was published, presenting at last an insider's view of the clubs and readings in which this movement had taken place. It is a frank and entertaining account of social change in this significant locale. It relies heavily on an anecdotal, often overtly documentary-type tone, and Cornelius's illustrations serve to place the 'greats' alongside ordinary Liverpudlians. The Beatles are depicted as totally ordinary, and the chapter dealing with the visit of a 'famous poet' is deliberately downbeat and unimpressed, while successfully monitoring the cultural milieu:

> 'That bloke over there,' muttered Keith *sotto voce*, 'is a famous poet. But don't look now.' He'd lapsed back into his own accent now, moving onto a different topic.[9]

The book gives an enlightening account of the art-college student scene, the clubs, the petty crooks, the drugs, and poetry events as an integral, unquestioned part of the night life. Cornelius mentions the divisive, violent attitudes that lead to 'hippy bashing', and acknowledges that, to a certain extent, even in Liverpool 8 not all poets were free from their audience's prejudicial opinions.

Cornelius includes poetry alongside songs and communal entertainment. For instance, in his account of O'Connor's bar, poetry is treated with respect:

> But mostly the place was full to capacity with jostling, strangely-clad figures, the majority of whom were zonked out of their skulls on a variety of illegal substances. Upstairs, slightly more restrained and avant-garde music and poetry evenings were held regularly, catering mainly for the student element.[10]

Cornelius singles out Mike Hart, 'a singer of down-and-out appearance but great ability' who 'performed regularly at O'Connor's'.[11] He sketches Hart playing guitar, with two pints of beer lined up and a carrier bag by one leg. There is a look of immense satisfaction on his face.

Even more indicative of the absolute pleasure prompted by a comfortable and welcoming audience is the drawing of 'A Poetry Reading'. On the wall is a notice: 'Hope Hall Poetry Reading: Adrian Henri, Roger McGough, Mike Hart, Mike Evans, Andy Roberts', and the illustration shows a massive Henri holding forth, with guitar and saxophone accompaniment, while in the background McGough stands waiting his turn in a caricature of the Scaffold image.[12] Cornelius presents poetry in Liverpool as being democratised, egalitarian, integrated with its audience and massively self-confident in its purpose.

Stuck in Stereotypes?

In researching this book, it slowly dawned on me that the tendency of the media and the literary establishment to talk about 'the Mersey poets' has created certain expectations, and has also limited the definition to the McGough–Patten–Henri triumvirate. For instance, Phil Bowen's book *A Gallery to Play To* (1999) is subtitled 'The Story of the Mersey Poets', but deals only with those three writers. This is not a criticism, in the sense that Bowen's express purpose had been to write only about those three. However, the shortcoming becomes apparent when one comes to consider other writers who happen to be living and working in Liverpool and have the accent, delivery, intonation and so on of the triumvirate. There is a stereotype of 'the Liverpool poet', and this mythic figure may be doing a disservice to other writers in the city – those who stayed behind as it were after the export of the defined 'attitude'. Of course, this attitude is one of the sustaining strengths of the poets who left, and, of course, they often write about Liverpool and their roots there. Perhaps the label is inescapable, just as terms such as 'Anglo-Irish' and 'Anglo-Welsh' will always create dissent.

What, then, are the significant questions? What issues need to be raised about poetry in non-metropolitan Britain, and Liverpool in particular? The essays here aim to describe rather than analyse, but they contain some surprises, and these illustrate how formidable is our stress on London as the poetic centre. This point is reinforced when one considers other regional identities in poetry. The fact is that, in England, we have never attained that solid regional base for the publication and dissemination of poetry that is to be found for instance in Wales. There have been small blocks such as the Dymock poets or the writers who gather around regional magazines such as Peter Sansom's *The North*, but in Liverpool there was something perhaps unique, though it lasted for only a decade, at least in its media-created form.

What about writing in the city since the 1970s? Some of the contributors here make it clear that, although the inevitable process of mass-media anonymity has removed a certain communal focus for writing, nevertheless the groups go on and poets of ability are produced. Also, significant poets have been connected with Liverpool and found the city to be a source of material, if not inspiration. Notably, Adrian Henri and Matt Simpson have stayed and become local *eminences grises* of the art.

It is difficult to reach any confident conclusions about this social context over the last three decades, but a few elements are worth reiterating. First, Liverpool gave poetry in general a sense of the centrality of the art to the popular spirit. Its writers made poetry as important as the strongest emotions. The poems contained in the Liverpool anthologies also demonstrated that there was no subject beyond the scope of poetry. *The Mersey Sound* was successful largely because it related to poetry as a celebration of the emotions fundamental to our language and being. It was never literary and ignored the literary canon.

The most difficult question is: How exactly did Liverpool itself contribute to this process? It may be that Patten's rise to success gives some of the answer. The story of his magazine *Underdog* is, in miniature, an account of these confident, relentless artistic assertions. It was only a small magazine on the fringes of the student circuit, but it contained work by the Beats, displayed French Symbolist influences, and had no inferiority complex. If it had a manifesto, it was that poetry was worthy of attention because it was an art expressive of our sharpest, most human experiences.

Time may well prove Liverpool poetry to be as significant as other well-grounded and better-financed metropolitan groups. What is certain is that the city has continued to provide stimulation through its recurrent contrasts and contradictions. In the popular imagination it is associated with the Toxteth riots, but also with the impressive Albert Dock and the iconic television soap *Brookside*. It is popularly believed to be a spawning ground for 'hard men', and its culture is still predominantly working class in popular myth; a city of sacred football, ferries and twanging guitars. When Julie Goodyear, the actress most famous as the barmaid Bet Lynch in *Coronation Street*, was chosen as a cultural ambassador for Liverpool in 1998, Adrian Henri was prompted to defend his city. He provided a wealth of impressive examples of artists connected with it, but his lament was 'Liverpudlians from George Stubbs to George Melly have adorned British culture. So why do we have such a lousy image?' He finds the answer, paradoxically, in 1963 'when "Love Me Do" echoed from the nation's first transistor radios.'[13] Yet together with that came the new poetry, established well before 1963, although admittedly it came second to pop music in terms of media representation. The appeal is in the people themselves, in the products of such a fusion of races. As Patten says, such things had already been used as source material in the street songs. The subject matter was just waiting for a more structured and formally educated generation.

Along with this repositioning of poetry as an accessible mode of popular cultural writing came a reappraisal of the notion of performance poetry; while never specifically addressed here, the subject is always at the base of the enquiries conducted in this book. It is hard to deny, despite some practitioners' dislike of the term 'performance poet', that the Liverpool writers influenced the ways in which we see performance now; they helped us to understand that a verbal text has to be realised in its moment of life – that is, with each re-reading.

I hope that this book encourages devotees of contemporary poetry to re-read Liverpool writing; such work did not cease when McGough and Patten moved away. I am also certain that some of the criticisms of 'pop' poetry, as exemplified by Norman Nicholson, will now appear way off the mark:

> Directness, spontaneity, informality, the lively image, the quick, arresting phrase, wit and humour, can all help to make a poem enjoyable and effective – but they don't make a poem in themselves. The trouble with much pop poetry is that it is too spontaneous!'[14]

References

1 'Keep your charity to yourselves – we are proud to be Scousers', *Daily Mail*, 2 October 1998.
2 Howard Channon, *Portrait of Liverpool*, London, Hale, 1970, p. 100.
3 Vitaly Vitaliev, 'Baedeker raids', *Daily Telegraph*, 26 June 1999.
4 Spencer Leigh, 'Obituary for Brian O'Hara', *The Times*, 16 June 1999.
5 Edward Lucie-Smith, *The Liverpool Scene*, London, Donald Carroll, 1967, p. 5.
6 Lucie-Smith, *The Liverpool Scene*, p. 6.
7 Lucie-Smith, *The Liverpool Scene*, p. 46
8 See Walter J. Ong, *Orality and Literacy*, London, Routledge, 1992, pp. 31–75.
9 John Cornelius, *Liverpool 8*, London, John Murray, 1982; repr. Liverpool, Liverpool University Press, 2001, p. 29.
10 Cornelius, *Liverpool 8*, p. 36.
11 Cornelius, *Liverpool 8*, p. 37.
12 Cornelius, *Liverpool 8*, p. 38.
13 Adrian Henri, 'Sorry gerl, you just won't do', *The Guardian,* 10 September 1998.
14 Norman Nicholson, introduction to F. E. S. Finn (ed.), *Poems of the Sixties*, London, John Murray, 1976, p. vii.

Liverpool at the Millennium

Matt Simpson

City of arrivals, departures,
of comings and goings,

your character determined by
the choppy ebb and flow of tides,

sailings and shore-leave,
signings on and off,

one day securing ropes,
the next day slipping them:

your come-day-go-day
perky Scouse philosophy

comes from rattling gangplanks,
shifting decks: a jauntiness

derived from old habits
of rolling home, then, skint,

of sailing off again. Your fortunes tidal,
you rise and fall in prosperity

like barometer mercury. No wonder,
for insurance, you flaunt not one but two

pert phoenixes above your waterfront,
one backwards staring, the other dead ahead,

plonk two grandiose cathedrals,
one space-age, the other antwacky,
at opposite ends of a street
called Hope. No wonder

you heroically support
two footie teams, the Reds, the Blues,

whose fortunes also rise and fall
like Mersey's grey-brown tides.

No wonder reconciliation, co-existence
are themes you nag away at,

shifting as you always do
between swagger and uncertainty.

Here's another Big Ben moment then
for taking stock, sussing things out properly,

one that marks two thousand Christian years,
in which you just about half-share

(that's if we all agree the kick-off's
twelve-O-seven with King John).

So let this moment be bright and brash
with celebration,

with fireworks and fanfares,
lashings of lobscouse,

and god-bless-yer-owld-cotton-socks,
Liverpool,

breeder of saints and sinners, of bruisers
and jesters and backstreet poets.

It's time to think again in terms
not of fall but rise – right for us

to think less of murky Merseyside and more
of resurgent Liverpool, time to be sexy

like that rude statue on Lewis's
where all the lovers meet.

(Commissioned by Liverpool City Council)

Streets of Hope

Levi Tafari

Stereotypes
media hypes
the victim Liverpool

They painted a picture
of a criminal culture
uncouth and very, very cruel

In vibrant times
poets created rhymes
and comedians carried the swing

There was Merseybeat
the vibe out on the street
Yeah! Everybody wanted to sing

'You'll never walk alone
In my Liverpool home'
LFC wore the colours of success

They would beat teams up
while retaining the cup
teams who visited left distressed

Check out the TV soap
visit the Street of Hope
with two cathedrals shrouded in fame

Newspapers from the gutter
distorted the disaster
Liverpool was back in the frame
I know people love the accent

but then some pass judgement
that Scousers are always on the rob

There is a Scouser in town
so screw everything down
if you're a Scouser you can't get a job

Some visit the Albert Docks
close to the Liver Clocks
and sail the ferry across the Mersey

Check out the famous skyline
recognised every time
with an image that is Oh! So chirpy

Well she is known worldwide
this daughter of Merseyside
with a passion that burns like fire

So the reason I write
is to shed forth some light
and Liverpool you never fail to INSPIRE

1

LITERARY MATTERS

The Arrival of McGough

Stephen Wade

Back in Liverpool in 1953 after university, Roger McGough was well placed to see the link between the kind of humorous poetry that the Hull student newspaper had liked and the more strident and incisive work of Christopher Logue, whose writing had so impressed him compared with the more intellectual poetry he had met both at school and again in the literary circles of the university and its magazine. Logue had produced his poems as posters, for instance, and written for *Private Eye*. When McGough was a student in Hull, trying to get his work published, Philip Larkin wrote in reply to some work that McGough had sent to him, and gave an encouraging response to some poems; this clearly had an impact, as McGough has commented in interviews. There was no lack of self-belief, when, in 1958, he also discovered the Beats and particularly Jack Kerouac.

Not much has been written about the influences behind McGough's writing, which he took up between the end of the 1950s and 1962, when his group Scaffold was formed. The popular assumption, reinforced by McGough's image on stage and television, is that he was a 'sixties poet', and the cover photographs on his early volumes suggest that he was 'a style guru', as he has playfully remarked.[1] On the cover of *Gig* (1973), a collection reflecting life on the road and the poetry circuit, he wears a dark hat, a beard and a necktie, a bohemian image which reflected the fashion of the period. But before this, he had been learning his craft from a wide range of literary sources, and one of the distinguishing features of the poetry of *The Mersey Sound* volume of 1967 is that many of the stylistic effects are non-literary. Jack Kerouac and the American Beats, well before the 1960s, had portrayed a sense of awe and admiration in the sheer flow of spontaneous writing that led to *On The Road* – after a good editor had been to work on it, of course. McGough refers specifically to the notion of seeing that poetry could be accessible, and

that form may be secondary to rhythms and structures from an emo-
tional centre and a poetic discourse of directness. He had found this in
his reading of Christopher Logue, perhaps because there is a certain for-
eign influence in Logue's work; Logue had also written songs for a
nightclub, so he was already breaking down barriers between discrete
forms of poetry.

It should also be recalled that, since his first poem was published in
Tomorrow magazine (1959) while he was still at college, McGough had
started writing long, symbolic poetry in the style of Rimbaud (so his
French studies at Hull were not all in vain, despite the lectures in French
which he jokingly says he couldn't understand). The fact is that
McGough had seen what Rimbaud's towering imagery could achieve,
and obviously tried to build a narrative in the same style; he was also
influenced by the spontaneity and energy of Kerouac and, to a lesser
extent, Allen Ginsberg. He took back to Liverpool, then, a strong desire
to write poetry that would be understood and would entertain, yet
would also say something important.

The Rimbaudesque poems were 'visionary and quasi-religious'
(McGough's own words), and his enjoyment and satisfaction with this
early writing clearly provided him with the will to write, and with the
certainty that writing was his vocation. In his 20s, he says, he was 'trying
to communicate with everybody. I've been trying to do that all my life.'

When eventually (in the early 1960s) he gathered like-minded
writers and musicians around him and started planning events and
gigs, he insists that there was never a sense of a crusade, but at one time
there was an agenda. The younger Brian Patten now entered the scene,
and Adrian Henri was very much involved with the projects. Patten was
to become a journalist for the *Bootle Times* in 1961, and his need to write
passionately autobiographical poems was in keeping with the mood of
the times; his enthusiasm in these early days was remarkable.
McGough recalls that Henri would make sets and posters for the first
readings in cafes, pubs and clubs around Liverpool. The readings were
mixed-media affairs, often at Hope Hall, but there were also 'happen-
ings' that said a great deal about the impulses behind the writing. These
were based on Jasper Johns's 'happenings', and involved rock 'n' roll
and a good knees-up. The three poets wrote a 'Mersi-festo' and the
tenor of this was to bring joy and celebration to words. It was exciting.
McGough remembers that 'You would grab at anybody who was famous
– we were desperate for heroes and wanted to put Liverpool on the
map.'

McGough also came home in need of a job, of course, and started teaching at St Kevin's RC secondary school in Kirkby, where he worked for two years before moving on to the Mabel Fielder Technical College where he taught French for the catering profession; but teaching did not appeal to him. School, after all, had been an unpleasant experience for him and although he had always been good at English, the only positive aspects he had taken from the educational experience were a confidence in delivering poetry, being rhetorical and dramatic, and a feeling for painting and colour. He went to evening classes at Liverpool College of Art and studied drawing. Behind this was a passion for Surrealism, something that he had also enjoyed in the poetry of Jacques Prevert. He had studied Latin at school in place of art, but the visual dimension in his imagination had always been strong. He has executed illustrations, notably to accompany the poems in the 1977 reprint of his collection *Sporting Relations* (the artwork in the 1974 edition was by Terry Gilliam).

The years from 1958 to 1962, before the launch of his pop and television career, are particularly fascinating. He talks about 'writing dialogues' for the readings in which there was always a special kind of irreverence, mixed with the desire to avoid solemn, well-trodden satirical paths. The real clue to understanding how the freshness and vigour of *The Mersey Sound* poetry came about is in the poet and critic Edward Lucie-Smith's ground-breaking book of soundbites, impressions and photographs, *The Liverpool Scene* (1967). Produced at the point when Scaffold were at their peak and McGough had proved himself to be an impressive all-rounder in the media world, the book gives a fascinating insight into this milieu. McGough has a lot to say about the audience, and this is the central factor here, the determinant of this unique piece of literary history. He says, 'In Liverpool you're a poet one minute, but the next minute you're talking about football, or you're buying bus tickets, or someone's kicking your head in down at the Blue Angel.' Even more interesting is his statement about the poets' identity and about the context: 'We've got no literary or dramatic heritage. We try out what we're doing, and we test it on people, and people react, and we sort of go on from there. We haven't got people to bow down to.' In other words, there were certain situations which were the product of a confluence of often paradoxical sources, some educational and some cultural.

This is at the heart of McGough's rise to success in these years. While many young poets were deeply bookish and well tutored in cerebral approaches to the classical study of English literature, McGough and his circle were in touch with life though the senses and through immediate contact with people, and were very much aware of a specific community of people, drawing on visible social roots and expressions of identity. This is not to say that McGough was ignorant of technique and of poetic convention. He has always been interested in formal qualities, and in the arrangement of poems in sequence, as in a 'set' for a reading. A cruel comment by Clive James about 'the great unwashed' of Liverpool serves to highlight a growing rift between McGough's group and the self-conscious intelligentsia who had been exposed to the disciplines of the great literary critic F. R. Leavis and the serious treatment of poetry as a crafted artefact. Lucie-Smith's book makes it clear that the Liverpool community was openly and innocently unliterary, and that poetry had the potential to take its place in 'pop' culture, which would make it indistinguishable from so-called 'lowbrow' culture. In fact, the new Mersey poets revelled in being lowbrow, interpreting this as a new kind of writing rather than something determinedly anti-aesthetic. The photographs in *The Liverpool Scene* identify this community more easily with run-down urban areas in the US than with the culture-soaked cities in the UK, where university campuses and English departments manage poetry readings in polite outlets, mainly for 'cultured' people. In one photograph McGough and Henri slouch at the window of a cafe, as a sign behind them proclaims 'Batman Cometh with Steak and Kidney Pies'. This even contains an in-joke, as Batman was a motif frequently used by the Liverpool poets, fitting in with their humour of childhood simplicity and self-mockery. In another, Henri, chubby and Beatnik, stares vacantly at the camera, the background being a heart-shaped piece of graffito with a question mark to the left. The clothes and the streets reflect the sparseness, austerity and bareness of a monochrome microcosm into which poetry is about to burst like a firework, dazzling with power and joy. The in-jokes used by Liverpool writers at the time – like Batman and Superman – were simply metaphors for the power of childhood as an imaginative presence in the poetic voice.

As McGough has written in an article in the *Daily Mail* (2 October 1998), the sense of identity in Liverpool is very much moulded by a peculiar geography. He talks about a community at a distance from any other city, facing the sea, and with a sprinkling of Irish and Welsh inhabitants; this community needs to create humour out of itself, to make fun of its own ways and attitudes. 'Liverpool was at once the centre of the world – and a backwater. It is a contradiction, but any place worth anything is a contradiction', he writes. One bedrock of this community was the famed Scouse wit. McGough's working-class family, together with his realisation that poetry was one way to use wit and self-deprecation in order to make an impact, played prominent roles in his success story.

McGough's concept of poetry was formed by this confluence of high and low art. Kerouac and the Beats, together with Rimbaud and Baudelaire, had provided a view of poetry as rebellion, and also as documentary. Poetry could log an experience, whether it was a nocturnal walk or the sight of the faces of the suffering poor. His working-class family and ideology had provided him with the usual view of poetry as being far removed from anything that could be called 'work'. In fact McGough says of this milieu, 'If you're a poet, it's something to be ashamed of...'

In Liverpool 8, Streate's coffee bar was one of the focal points of this vibrant new culture. Perhaps the best-known account of this area is in Henri's poem 'Liverpool 8': it is a 'once-fashionable Georgian district now scrawled over with graffiti, scarred with unhealed bomb-sites, dominated by the stranded neo-Gothic whale of the Anglican cathedral.' The audience at the time would also find at Streate's some London-based writers such as Pete Brown and Spike Hawkins. The basement club and other pub venues indicate the nature of the audience that McGough refers to when he says, 'At the readings we did ... the kids didn't look on it as Poetry with a capital P, they looked on it as modern entertainment. They may go away crying or go away sad, but it was a certain experience for them, all part of experience.'

Johnny Byrne, an Irishman who was part of the group and who knew Adrian Henri, commented in Lucie-Smith's book that McGough and Patten were unknown, and that 'Roger and Brian just turned up at respective times when we were there and asked if they could read...' It is evident that the general atmosphere of experimentation and togetherness in the poetry grew alongside the boom in pop culture and the 'invention of the teenager', as sociologists have referred to it. These teenagers may have been in need of direction; they were certainly in need of distraction and entertainment, and pop poetry was part of their scene. McGough's reflections on his art at the time emphasise an approach to language and writing that demystifies. He was never into theoretical talk about methodology. His first real success, and a lasting one, was *Summer with Monika*, and an interesting insight is given by the text and also by the illustrations that were produced by Peter Blake for the reprint in 1978. This is a narrative that devalues the dominance of the directing self. It uses throwaway lines and mundane colloquial language to embellish a love story. McGough's reading of e. e. cummings, with his disregard of punctuation, is a factor in this effect; and it is also documented that McGough, from his childhood, had a habit of speaking too quickly. Thus his trademark styles of running words together, ignoring punctuation at times, and destroying clichés in order to create freshness, are all here.

> Somedays we thought about the seaside
> And built sandcastles on the blankets
> And paddled in the pillows
> Or swam in the sink…

This volume also contains some of the first attempts at 'kinetic' or 'concrete' poetry, in which McGough makes the text active and increases reader interest by means of typographical tricks (using differing font sizes or perspective, for instance). In other words, his need to entertain and his knowledge of the locality and audience perhaps provided more assurance when it came to experimenting. After all, the art on record covers (particularly on albums and extended play recordings) was making similar appeals to young people, but the traditionally 'serious' world of poetry was excluded from these concerns before the Underground and the Mersey Sound (see below) appeared (not that McGough and his contemporaries were aware of being a 'movement' at this early stage).

As the readings and happenings became more frequent, McGough developed his image. He was to become a smooth operator in these years, organising and planning the performances; and appearance, dramatic stance and intonation were crucial to his success. The literary setting was what came to be referred to as 'Underground'. Michael Horovitz produced the anthology *Children of Albion* in 1969, and it purported to be 'poetry of the Underground'. Although this is difficult to define, it was certainly anti-establishment and placed class and political factors at the centre of its agenda. The Mersey Poets were not included in that anthology, and McGough did not take part in the Albert Hall Poetry Incarnation, also in 1969; but there are parallels between this movement and McGough's work, the main one being that this species of poetry depends entirely on rapport with and knowledge of the audience. McGough's professionalism in this respect appeared early in his career.

A photograph in Lucie-Smith's book shows him reading, wearing dark glasses and a corduroy suit, with curly hair and throwing an expressive gesture. He stands by a mike. Everything about the image contradicts the traditional view of a poetry reading. He was always aware of the dullness of a reading in which the poet doesn't care about the audience, where he or she 'just opens a book and reads'. In these years, before the musical developments which lead to Scaffold, he learned about being sensitive to the audience's reactions, about feedback and the use of appropriate humour. He has always arranged a set – an order of reading – so that the structure is apparent, and most importantly, offers subjects that have an appeal for everyone. A democratisation of the poetic discourse itself, removing it from that mythical, sacerdotal status which relates to hushed silences and revered listening to the 'bard' whose words are somehow separate from the words used in the street when buying bread or talking about the family. Kerouac had done this while managing to heighten the rhythms and diction into lyrical beauty and pathos, mixing them successfully. McGough was working to mix the inspirational and the passionate with the mechanical mundanity of life as it is lived, not as it is imaged.

In 1962 there was to be a new focus for all this energy, which grew naturally from local cabaret and readings and from the further advancement of the Liverpool identity into Scaffold. At the Mersey Arts Festival, John Gorman, 'a real motivator' (McGough), assembled talent from a range of artistic interests. These included Mike McCartney (who was to be Mike McGear in the group), Michael Weinblatt (a hairdresser) and Arthur Dooley (a sculptor). The enterprise used a jokey letterhead under the name of Mike Blank, and their material had been developed in the clubs. McGough would open with a reading, then there would be a balanced scripted programme, and a series of dialogues from McGough. Other people involved included Jennifer Beattie and Adrian Henri. McGough recalls that 'the TV [people] were around at the time – and we conceived this routine where John was the "Scouser" and I was the gent'. The various shows were given tongue-in-cheek names such as the *Liverpool One Fat Lady All Electric Show* ('one fat lady' referring to the '8' of Liverpool 8). The big break came with the group's appearance on the ABC *Saturday Night* programme. Other television appearances included *Tonight* with Cliff Michelmore, which was recorded in the Manchester studios and which featured the dancer Carol Mason alongside McGough, who 'sat on a ladder and read poems'. Henri did some set-painting. McGough calls the effect a mixture of mythology and play.

Scaffold, named by McGough, was alive and thriving. By the time of their appearances on *Gazette* in 1964, he had stopped teaching completely and was undoubtedly a professional writer.

Gazette, hosted by Jim Lloyd, made intense demands on McGough as a writer and entertainer. The driving force behind this development was the director and 'trainer' of the band, Clive Goodwin. Scaffold auditioned and were one of three groups who were chosen to feature on the show, whose catchphrase became 'Famous in the North'. The live programme ran for a 13-week season, and featured guests such as Barry Humphries, *Them, The Spencer Davies Group*, Lulu and *The Kinks*. McGough notes that 'Our job was to do a sketch and ad lib'. Newspapers were left on the seats in the studio, and the performances would be based on items in these papers. The experience sharpened his ability to think quickly and create witty observational humour.

This programme catapulted McGough into the limelight. His poetry writing continued and the Brecht scholar, John Willett, found McGough an agent, Pat Burke, and even a voice teacher in Golder's Green a little later on. This latter point is a quite significant fact upon which McGough has commented. As has been noted by critics, he had received some elocution lessons as a child, but this later episode was more important. He says, 'We went down to London to learn how to become luvvies', and 'by the end of a fortnight we still had our own accents and our teacher was speaking broad Scouse.' It was all happening for the provincial man with a feel for a local audience; he was having to adapt to a mass-media audience, and was under tremendous pressure to meet deadlines.

The Scaffold concept and name refers to the group's habit of dressing as executioners, wearing black gloves and a variety of loud ties with the lugubrious outfits. They went into revue, appeared in a show at the Traverse in Edinburgh called, whimsically, 'Birds, Marriages and Deaths'. The Beatles' manager Brian Epstein became their agent at this point, yet as McGough admits, they 'never had a game plan'. He notes that they may have suffered through this lack; they took whatever was on offer. They had become alternative comedians, running parallel to other traditions such as the Cambridge Footlights revues. Their song 'Lily the Pink' got to number one in 1968, but before that, they had established a format for cabaret which had less poetry and more music. McGough even found time to spend three weeks with the playwright Charles Marowitz at the Open Space working on 'The Puny Little Life Show', a piece which involved no music, and ran for three weeks.

A slight deviation was occasioned by McGough's appearance on the cover of the *Radio Times* in 1966 as 'new actor of the year'. This was for his work as narrator on *Saturday While Sunday*, directed by Jim Goddard. He had also been voted 'most promising newcomer' by the critic at the *Daily Express*. The cast also included Michael Pennington, Malcolm McDowell and Tim Dalton. It seemed at the time as though a new career was on offer, and this became a crisis point for him; his relationship was breaking down, and the demands of writing in so many diverse contexts at the same time were taking their toll. Scaffold began to break up and he had many other options that offered potential outlets for his skills in comedy and poetry. It was plain that he was a cabaret performer in a sense, but with a second career as a poet of increasing stature. However, his work did not expand any further into other roles.

1967 was without doubt an *annus mirabilis* for McGough, who enjoyed an incredible deluge of work and success. Edward Lucie-Smith published *The Liverpool Scene* and Penguin published *The Mersey Sound*. Scaffold appeared at the Everyman Theatre with guests including a poetry-rock band led by Adrian Henri. McGough's first play, *The Commission*, was performed at the Everyman Theatre in Liverpool, and Michael Joseph published both his novel, *Frink*, and the narrative poem *Summer with Monika*.

There were also some failures, despite the fact that the media obviously believed that here was a writer who could turn his hand to any task. He was involved in some writing for the film *Yellow Submarine*, and even given the chance to work on an unfinished screenplay by Joe Orton. He was invited to do this by Richard Lester, and McGough describes how he was given an office and all the support he wanted. But it wasn't right at the time and he turned it down. It would have been the end of Scaffold if he had taken it up.

McGough was earning his living by lecturing after Scaffold's first successes, yet in July 1967 musical recording was to figure in some radical changes in his life. 'Scaffold seemed to be falling apart with my increasing appearances on television and at poetry performances', McGough comments. On 29 July that year McGough made, in his own phrase, a rare excursion into London's Swinging Sixties when Scaffold appeared at the 'Love-In' at the Alexandra Palace. Acts included the Crazy World of Arthur Brown, and there was a photograph of John Gorman and McGough accompanying a *News of the World* article that described 'drug-crazed-hippies in sex orgy'. McGough was unaware of anything so sensational taking place, and calls the article a fabrication. The pinnacle of Scaffold's success was reached with their appearances on such programmes as *Top of the Pops* and *Dee Time* with 'Thank You Very Much', released on 4 November. McGough says that this success brought new life into the Scaffold enterprise and that it 'pulled me away from a solo career'.

Scaffold declined slightly in popularity after this, but McGough's work with the Bonzo Dog Doo-Dah Band began. The shows with comedy, poetry and guests continued, and the group Grimms, a combination of Scaffold and Bonzo personnel, was formed. The acronym was for Gorman, Innis, McGough, McGear and (Vivien) Stanshall. The thrill was derived from unpredictability and surreal play. 'People would throw jelly-babies at us', he recalls.

Subsequently, Scaffold was revived and McGough's habit of writing on the move continued. The lyrics of 'Lily the Pink' were written on a train on the way to Abbey Road studios, for instance; and the poems in the collection *Watchwords* exemplify the kind of subjects and styles being worked on at this time. The editor and agent Ed Victor was part of this project at the publisher Cape, and his attraction to the project lay partly in the fact that this was a book of poems written at speed, resulting in an air of readiness and directness mixed with the crazy anti-boredom themes and surreal indulgences of the songs. McGough insists, though, that he did differentiate between writing for immediate performance, and poems produced for more careful readings. *Watchwords* grew from this programme of wit on the move.

McGough's role on the BBC programme *Eleventh Hour*, conceived by Anthony Smith of Magdalene College, characterises his way of life at this time. The programme was based on a panel of four, and McGough's role was to write a poem a week for the audience. On the day of the show he would be 'shut in a dressing room and told to write – a poem that would last two minutes forty seconds or one that might last three minutes fifty seconds!' The show also included Richard Neville, Ray Davies and Miriam Margolies.

McGough's reflections on the quality of this mid-1960s writing and its critical reception typify his attitude to the integrity of his craft, particularly his musings on whether or not he would have been a more 'valued' poet had he specialised in poetry in a conventional sense, publishing slim volumes and work in anthologies. In fact, this question has been so prevalent that he and Brian Patten wrote a play about it called *The Mouth Trap*, staged at the Hammersmith Lyric theatre in the 1980s. The theme was the waste of time, but McGough is philosophical. 'You've got to have real life as well... the poetry was always there.'

In the background of the Liverpool movement there were strong cos-mopolitan leanings, in spite of the anti-Eng Lit and anti-establishment mood. One manifestation of this was Adrian Henri's interest in the French dramatist Alfred Jarry and his grotesque creation, Père Ubu. There was also something, perhaps what Patten called the 'hard lyric', that came from the sense of Liverpool as a frontier city, a wild location of forgotten industrialism that was post-boom and embedded in old-fashioned Labour values. The urge to follow enthusiasms wholeheart-edly and the disregard for established hierarchies of art were also important. The self-referential fun of Henri in his *Père Ubu in Liverpool* exemplifies a great deal about this unique achievement. Ubu meets a Liverpool 'bird' and, after some dialogue in which high-flown diction meets Scouse, Ubu says: 'Hornsgodouille, shittr, can no one here speak a civilised tongue?'

McGough was aware of this need to use the local identity as a differ-entiating feature. His first delight was in writing short dialogues, and these show the same love of paradox and nonsense as Henri's Ubu, as one of them, 'Flood', demonstrates. The theme is: Who would you be if you were not yourself? Each reply is more immensely imagistic than the last, as in 'If I wasn't me I'd be the worst flood for years'; the poem fin-ishes with an inconsequential reference to Vera Lynn. This is like the conversations had by lovers in the excitement of a new relationship, or the direct, unmannered chat of friendship, and McGough's early poems are concerned with this. They share the pop culture interest in senti-ment fused with satirical or whimsical impressionism. At the base of it all is the teenage feeling of a new freedom, an awareness that life offers pleasure and adventure, and that the working-class centre of a great seaport can become magical through language – the moribund language of survival and bland functional interchanges could become poetic, dynamic and vibrant.

This is the essence of McGough's achievement: he established him-self as a distinctive voice among many new players during the 1960s. What was particularly special about his progress, among the ranks of working-class youths who made it to university after the war, is that he found his source of imaginative sustenance at home. The cosmopolitan element mentioned above enriched this even further, and McGough's collaborations with Patten, together with his confidence in working with old friends such as Henri, placed a comet in poetry's sky just when it was most needed.

'I write poetry in various ways,' McGough has said, 'either the word or the image or the idea... A line starts me off – say a line like 'Monika the tea things are taking over.'... I never think of the poems in terms of performance, but I sometimes think... that this will be dramatic.' The years between leaving Hull and seeing *The Mersey Sound* in print are years in which he created a dramatic persona for himself. This was so versatile and multi-faceted that he was marked out as the poet who could produce work quickly and professionally and yet be seen as fundamentally 'underground'. That he saw himself as distant from the metropolitan centre in London is evidence that he was, initially at least, as much a regional writer as those dialect poets who form the long Lancashire tradition, stretching back to Edwin Waugh and Samuel Laycock in the Victorian period. Yet McGough emerged at a time when mass culture helped to create a poetry that would lose its sacred status and search without self-consciousness for voices in the demotic and vernacular.

By 1967, McGough had won a place in several cultural contexts, and his wit and adaptability were to revolutionise both his own life and poetry in general. In an interview with him in September 1998, it was clear that he was not really aware of just how profoundly the audience he gathered at this time has been moved, influenced and motivated as readers of poetry by the Mersey Sound revolution.

Note

1   All direct quotations from McGough are from an interview with the author in September, 1998.

The Hard Lyric

Re-registering Liverpool Poetry

Peter Barry

Contemporary poetry is in trouble. An indication of the depth of the malaise was given by Oxford University Press's attempt to cancel its poetry list at the end of 1998, on the grounds of its insufficient profitability.[1] Another symptom, which will be familiar to those who teach contemporary poetry at university, is the comparatively low take-up of degree-level poetry courses whenever they are optional. The symptoms, then, are obvious enough, but what are the causes? A major one, I believe, is that poetry lacks street-cred, or to be more specific, *street*-cred. In other words, the experience that is explored in contemporary poetry is too seldom that of a city-dweller. Poetry still has plenty of country-lane-cred and farm-and-meadow-cred, thanks to writers like Seamus Heaney and Ted Hughes – poets undoubtedly distinguished in talent, but relatively narrow in range. The latter's career presented us with a procession of animals that went on for over 30 years. His last book, *Birthday Letters* (1998), won all the available prizes,[2] but the unique circumstances of its publication and the sensational nature of its subject matter mean that poetry in general can draw no comfort from this fact. Unless we can re-associate poetry with the urban experience, we may have to accept its demise or its dearth, if not, just yet, its death. The present essay is part of an ongoing project that attempts to re-establish the connection between poetry and the city,[3] and it focuses on work associated with one particular city that has already featured prominently in the history of contemporary poetry – albeit mostly as a kind of 'pop' annex to the mainstream.

Following the 'Liverpool scene' of the 1960s, the city's poetry hardly registered nationally as a distinct entity until the late 1990s, when newer poets associated with the city produced a considerable body of work. The variety of this new work contrasts strikingly with what was seen as the tonal homogeneity of the 1960s generation: but I want to

argue, first, that the homogeneity of that earlier work is often exagger-
ated, and that the linguistic register of the earlier generation was often
both extremely fluid and shifting *within* individual poems, and
markedly varied from poet to poet. Secondly, I want to suggest that the
newer poets, while differing just as much from one another, operate on
a larger stage. They are registering the impact on poetry of a more trou-
bled era in which industrial collapse, social conflict and contested
national and regional identities prevent the growth of that unques-
tioned, pervasive local rootedness which is seen in the earlier material.
I will make some attempt to relate my perception of these changes to
the shifting urban environment which provides the material for these
poems. This essay examines three poets from each era, although it
treats the two groups rather differently, using, in the main, just a
single representative poem from each of the three major 1960s
figures, and not making any direct, cross-generational poet-to-poet
comparisons.

The work of both generations, then, needs to be seen against a back-
drop of violently fluctuating civic fortunes. In the 1960s, following the
success of the Beatles, there was something of a cultural renaissance in
Liverpool, which led to an explosion of activity related to pop and folk
music, painting and poetry. In 1965, Allen Ginsberg famously declared
Liverpool to be 'at the present moment the centre of the consciousness
of the human universe',[4] and this period of cultural confidence and
optimism is epitomised by Adrian Henri's poetry collections *Tonight
at Noon* (1967) and *City* (1968); by the Penguin Modern Poets volume
The Mersey Sound (1967) which contained poetry by Henri, Roger
McGough and Brian Patten; and by *The Liverpool Scene,* the collection
of poetry and photographs edited by Edward Lucie-Smith (1967).
The Liverpool poetry of this period was widely regarded as performance
poetry, related to that of the American Beats and the cognate British
'Children of Albion'. It was associated with pop music and art happen-
ings rather than with mainstream British poetry, which was represented
by Larkin, Hughes, the 'Movement' poets, and senior figures Eliot
and Auden.

A significant exception to the vow of silence that the academic estab-
lishment seemed to have taken about the Liverpool scene was Jonathan
Raban's *The Society of the Poem*,[5] which examined recent and contempo-
rary poetry from an unusually broad social and literary-historical per-
spective (as his title implies), devoting a few highly critical pages to the
Liverpool poets. Raban saw them as working 'through regional groups

and poetry readings', intent on 'finding a speaking voice for the poem', but the result is a 'whimsically impoverished speech, an attempt to get a local, private, dispossessed language into verse, to talk straight, bypassing poetic convention, to the audience' (p. 116). The style, he says, is 'curiously bastardized', owing something to 'the ad-libbed backchat of the stand-up comic, something of the language of movie dialogue... and something to the mesmeric relationship between the pop singer and his public'. This accurately identifies some of the linguistic elements in the dialogic mix of 1960s Liverpool poetry, and Raban goes on to suggest that several of the poems are knowing, ironic reversals of set genres such as the *epithalamium*, the elegy, the ode, the nursery rhyme or the moral tale. However, in Raban's view this is undercut by inherent limitations of outlook and subject matter. Henri, McGough, Patten and Henry Graham, he says, have 'a tedious sentimentality directed variously at small children and pubic schoolgirls' (p. 117), and yet 'this determined childishness, the sustained *faux naif* pose, does release a speaking voice which is able to talk freely from inside its retardations'.

Raban's criticism cannot be entirely discounted but it is not quite the whole picture, for the voice in the poems, as well as possessing a distinct linguistic mobility that allows it to cross registers that are seldom combined in the same discursive structure, is often more culturally complex than Raban suggests. For instance, in 'Limestreetscene '64' McGough shifts register, and indeed genre, as the poem progresses. He begins with an apparently inconsequential denotation of the speaker's peregrinations through the urban scene, fiercely loco-specific and clearly addressed to a readership that is familiar with the streets and the buildings mentioned:

> Turned left into Lime Street
> felt small
> like a pelota ball
>
> St George's Hall
> black pantheonic
> like a coalman's wedding cake
> glows in the neonic
> presence of Schweppervescence
> and 'Guinness is Good for You'

Here the exotic and culturally specific pelota ball is puzzlingly chosen for use in the simile, rather than (say) the more familiar tennis ball. The difference seems at first to add little, in a way precisely analogous to the moment when Eliot's Prufrock expresses his sense of the triviality of his own life by saying 'I have measured out my life in coffee spoons' – why, the reader might wonder, doesn't he just say '*tea*spoons'? The answer is twofold, for the image is skilfully over-determined. First, coffee spoons are smaller than teaspoons, so the idea of smallness and triviality is given extra force. Secondly, coffee spoons are distinctly genteel in comparison with teaspoons, and they therefore evoke the social milieu in which Prufrock's life is lived out. McGough's pelota ball has the same kind of double-denotative charge: first, it is smaller than a tennis ball (just a little bigger than a golf ball, and weighing about four and a half ounces), and hence intensifies the notion of personal smallness; secondly, and in a more complex way, it has an effect equivalent to the coffee spoon in connoting gentility. 'Pelota' is the Spanish word for 'ball', and it is also the name of the Basque team-game version of handball (*pelota vasca* or 'Basque ball'). Just like Eliot's coffee spoon it is a social-status indicator, for the effect is, first, to construct a speaker (and hence, of course, an audience) of fairly wide education and awareness to whom this game is known; the *faux naif* air of which Raban complains is revealed to be, precisely and knowingly, just that, when it occurs in the linguistic vicinity of such exotic vocabulary. Secondly, it imparts a cosmopolitan air that cuts across the conventional notion of a provincial city as a place narrow in outlook (an association which, I think, underscores Raban's comments on the Liverpool poets). The poem goes on to mention such things as Irish linen, Chinese cafes and Viking whalers to suggest the cultural and ethnic complexity of the city.

These linguistically implied elements of cultural sophistication recur in the second verse; in the mid-1960s, St George's Hall (the Victorian neoclassical building of immense bulk that confronts visitors emerging from Lime Street Station) had not yet been sandblasted clean, and its 'black pantheonic' presence dominated most city-centre views of the period. Its Roman (rather than Greek) style is also used in the adjoining complex of buildings comprising the William Brown Library, the Walker Art Gallery and the Liverpool Museum, so the coinage 'pantheonic' (referring to the Pantheon in Rome) is historically, architecturally and culturally precise. As an element in a linguistic register, therefore, it is distinctly different from the next line, which describes the building as being 'like a coalman's wedding cake'. This juxtaposition slips from acrolect to basilect, as linguists say: that is, to the kind of street chat that coins an irreverent description of a building which has passed into local lore. This kind of humour might also typify the 'ad-libbed back-chat of the stand-up comic', noted by Raban, but it should be said that the comparison is visually precise: the old-fashioned layered wedding cake is typically square, sits on a pedestal or platform and uses fluted columns as supports, a description which more or less fits the building. The coinage 'pantheonic' is echoed by 'neonic' a couple of lines later, describing the display of neon advertising signs attached to the hotels and other buildings which then faced Lime Street Station. 'Neonic' is an ironic back-formation from the academic register of 'pantheonic', starkly juxtaposing a brash commercial present with an idealistic Victorian past (the neon signs spell out 'Schweppervescence' and 'Guinness is Good for You'). This is to draw attention to the cultural and linguistic complexities of McGough's register: one could not accurately say that the poem is either chatty or cultured, as it is a dialogic mixture comprising both elements.

McGough's city does contain more disturbing elements: for instance, there are portrayals of meaningless violence in his work, such as the random shooting in 'The Day Before Yesterday'; but the treatment is predominantly cartoon-like. Having been shot in the forehead by a complete stranger while innocently walking down Dale Street, the speaker's parenthetical reaction is that 'it was terribly embarrassing'; he stumbles bleeding into the Kardomah Cafe, and the poem settles into a satire against the pretensions of chic gentility, for the speaker is much concerned about ruining his new 'Raelbrook shirt & vertical-striped Italian jacket with brass buttons', and maintains decorum by slipping 'into the gentlemen's' (note the registerial precision involved in *not* calling it 'the gents') to give up the ghost with as little fuss as possible. Likewise, the threat of nuclear destruction is dealt with in McGough's work, but again the treatment is slickly counter-intuitive, as in 'At Lunchtime, A Story of Love' in which the speaker's opportunistic announcement of an impending nuclear strike merely leads to scenes of joyous public copulation on the bus. The 'panic' spreads, so that each day people take erotic advantage and 'pretended that the world was coming to an end at lunchtime'. The poem ends 'It still hasn't. Although in a way it has', a cursive, whiplash ending that reactivates and readjusts our sense of the whole poem. Again, then, the poem becomes a satire on the social conventions which keep people separate from one another and encased in their inhibitions. Notice that the scenario is essentially urban: it depends on the crowded commuter bus bringing people into the city for work each day, a social space of unusual intimacy in which strangers sit in close and frequent proximity to each other, but remain strangers.

Where McGough is overtly loco-specific, frequently mentioning actual locations and drawing closely on their cultural and social implications, Brian Patten's 1960s work was much less overtly anchored, even though among members of the Liverpool scene he expressed perhaps most clearly the explicit aim of putting the city into the poems. In the interview snips that punctuate the poems in *The Liverpool Scene* he says

> I've been trying to get something about the city into my poems. I'm amazed I'm on this, this city with winds and grass blowing through, and it's like being on a planet, and this planet is in this universe, and the clouds are going past me, you know. It's a fantastic feeling. I'm trying to get this in my poems. Mainly lyric, the hard lyric. (p. 63)

The detail of this remark would lead us to expect more conventional 'lyricism' in Patten's work, but it is, as he memorably says, the 'hard lyric', with a kind of underlying toughness, which is typified by 'Party Piece', one of his best and best-known poems, in which a couple make love after a chance encounter at a party. The poem ends:

> So they did,
> Right there among the Woodbines and Guinness stains,
> & later he caught a bus, and she a train,
> And all there was between them then
> Was rain.

This is remarkably well-behaved poetry, simultaneously obeying the typographic conventions of prose (it has standard punctuation) and verse (every line is capitalised). It makes tight use of rhetorical tropes such as zeugma ('the party-goers go out/ & the dawn creeps in'), neat metaphoric transfers ('let's unclip our minds'), a tight lexical and syntactical balance within the line which is reminiscent of Pope ('& later he caught a bus, and she a train'), and a concluding iambic pentameter within a rhyming couplet structure ('And all there was between them then/ Was rain'). The line break in the pentameter is perfectly placed to facilitate the slight pause in performance which will give exactly the right sense of pathos and finality, and the whole poem is wrought with a fine spareness and concision. As an example of contemporary, street-wise, troubadour mode this could hardly be bettered, and the tender-ness it expresses is credible, proper to the macho protagonist, and salting the lyric, so to speak, with hardness. This is Patten at his best: the verse is virtually allusion-free, and remarkably homogeneous in register, without the shifts of linguistic gear that are common in McGough. The verbal dexterity echoes McGough's but it is seldom used for humorous effect, and the argument that this kind of writing is wholly performance-dependent makes little sense.

Adrian Henri's techniques differed very markedly from those of the other two poets in the group. Henri, then as throughout his career, was closely tuned in to the European and American artistic avant-garde, encompassing Dada and Surrealism, Marcel Duchamp, major modernist artists such as Jasper Johns and Kurt Schwitters, contemporary 'happenings', the activities of political groups such as the Situationists, and conceptual art generally. His 'Summer Poem Without Words' typifies this ambience and is richly redolent of its artistic provenance.

(To be distributed in leaflet form to the audience: each poem should be tried within the next seven days.)

1. Try to imagine your next hangover.
2. Travel on the Woodside ferry with your eyes closed. Travel back with them open.
3. Look for a black cat. Stroke it. This will be either lucky or unlucky.
4. Find a plastic flower. Hold it up to the light.
5. Next time you see someone mowing a lawn smell the smell of freshly-cut grass.
6. Watch *Coronation Street.* Listen to the 'B' side of the latest Dusty Springfield record.
7. Sit in a city square in the sunlight. Remember the first time you made love.
8. Look at every poster you pass next time you're on a bus.
9. Open the *News of the World* at page 3. Read between the lines.
10. The next time you clean your teeth *think* about what you're doing.

This might be called a poetic statement rather than a poem, for there is an element of conceptual art in the notion of the poem without words: the actions that are actually performed will be the poem, rather than the words on the page, which are merely its specification – just as, in what was later known as 'Land Art' (associated with figures such as Richard Long and Robert Smithson) the artefact is a physical walk through a certain terrain rather than the adjustments to the landscape (piled stones, for instance) which are the material traces of the activity. The actions listed in the poem constitute a radical reclamation of the most ordinary aspects of day-to-day life, radically extending our conception of what the imagination is, in the manner advocated by the Situationist theorist Raoul Vaneigem, for whom 'poetry is the act which reverses the perspective'. He continues 'True poetry cares nothing for poems. In his quest for the Book, Mallarmé wanted nothing so much as to abolish the poem. What better way could there be of abolishing the poem than realizing it?'

> Human beings are in a state of creativity twenty-four hours a day. Once revealed, the scheming use of freedom by the mechanisms of domination produces a backlash in the form of an idea of authentic freedom inseparably bound up with individual creativity.[6]

Henri's poem seeks to embody the ideals of this august Shelleyean rhetoric: it seeks to abolish poetry in the conventional sense (hence it calls itself a poem without words) and re-embody it in the individual creativity evoked by Vaneigem's text. In doing this he seeks to stimulate the backlash of individual freedom against the 'scheming mechanisms of domination'. Likewise, the cultural artefacts that would be despised as inauthentic by High Modernists schooled by Adorno – a plastic flower, *Coronation Street*, Dusty Springfield, advertising posters, the *News of the World* – are here salvaged and embraced. They are recommended not so much for study as for contemplation. In reading between the lines of the newspaper we are not being asked to look for hidden or implied meanings, and much less the construction of cultural, gender and racial identities; we are being asked to see the blank spaces. Likewise, we must 'look' or 'hold' or 'watch' or 'listen' for those crystallisations of the quotidian flux of perception, in the spirit of Susan Sontag's 1966 essay *Against Interpretation*.[7] The plastic flower, for instance, is to be genuinely admired: in another of Henri's poems the first sign of spring is the appearance of plastic daffodils in Woolworths. The flower is not despised as inauthentic, nor – heaven forbid – regarded as a symptomatic simulacrum of the postmodern identity. Such puritanical condemnations are utterly remote from a sequence of observations that teases us out of thought with the relentlessness of Keats's 'cold pastoral' urn. Other lines in the sequence recommend experiencing the senses and bodily sensations (imagining a hangover, travelling with closed eyes). Such 'deep' experiencing of the simplest everyday act (brushing the teeth, for instance) is of the kind that Vaneigem sees as potentially transforming. It attempts to understand an oft-made proclamation – one which again teases us out of thought – that in a post-revolutionary situation literally *everything* would be different.

If we were to generalise, then, about the way the city suffuses and is represented by this 1960s verse, we could argue that it is an urban playground, always potentially the benign backdrop to the poet's pleasure, enlightenment and fulfilment. As the facilitator of the poet's experiential and personal odyssey, it becomes the urban equivalent of Wordsworthian 'nature' – a point to which I will return below.

If the 'pop' poetry of the 1960s voiced a confident, regionally devolved literature in a city still very sure of its worth and values, then the contrast with the poetry of the 1990s is very stark. Liverpool's cultural bubble burst in the 1970s and 1980s, and as industrial decline and civic demoralisation gathered pace, a series of widely reported disasters occurred that were associated with the city, including the riots in Toxteth in 1981, the Heysel Stadium tragedy involving Liverpool football fans in Brussels in May 1985, the Hillsborough disaster in Sheffield in April 1989 which again involved Liverpool fans, and the abduction and murder of two-year-old James Bulger in February 1993 by two ten-year-old boys. From 1983 to 1991 a Militant-dominated Labour administration under Derek Hatton made Liverpool synonymous in the national media with the extremes of left-wing local government. The cumulative demoralising effect on the city of these events is difficult to estimate but it was considerable, and undoubtedly suffuses the later poetry associated with the city.

A major source for Liverpool-based poetry in the 1990s is the anthology *Liverpool Accents: Seven Poets and a City*.[8] In one sense the book represents a kind of Liverpudlian poetic diaspora. Of the seven poets included, Elaine Feinstein was born in the city but grew up elsewhere; Grevel Lindop, a Professor of English at Manchester University, followed the academic Oxbridge path out of the city at 18; Jamie McKendrick spent part of his childhood there but is now Oxford-based; Deryn Rees-Jones was born in Liverpool, read English at Bangor, then took a doctorate at Birkbeck College before moving back to Liverpool to take up an academic post; Peter Robinson lived in Liverpool from the age of three, left to study at York and Cambridge universities, and has been an English lecturer in Japan for more than a decade; Adrian Henri, the only 1960s poet included, lived in Liverpool for over 40 years; and Matt Simpson was born in Bootle, studied at Cambridge, returned to Liverpool and has since carved out his career as an academic in the city.

However, although *Liverpool Accents* does not represent a strictly Liverpudlian group, it nevertheless represents some key aspects of Liverpool poetry in the 1990s just as *The Liverpool Scene* and *The Mersey Sound* represented the 1960s. The fact that the contributors to the later book are geographically scattered means that they are not generally in direct contact with a more-or-less homogeneous audience through readings and performances, as the 1960s poets were; that culture no longer exists.

The most sustained use of the city's landscape and environment is in the work of Matt Simpson, while the poet whose references to it are the most oblique and fragmentary is Deryn Rees-Jones, and I will therefore concentrate on the work of these two as a kind of bracketing pair (though not confining discussion to poems in *Liverpool Accents*). I will also discuss a work of a very different kind, Robert Hampson's sequence *Seaport*,[9] which was published, like so much poetry that has later emerged as significant, outside the spheres of mainline publishing houses and distribution networks.

Matt Simpson's main collections have all been published by Newcastle's Bloodaxe Books, beginning with *Making Arrangements* in 1982 (now out of print but included in *An Elegy for the Galosherman: New and Selected Poems*, 1990); his most recent collection to date is *Catching up with History* (1995). All Simpson's work draws closely on his personal experience and has a strong narrative thread that runs from poem to poem. As he says in the biographical note to *Galosherman*,

> Most of the poems in this collection have been carefully arranged so as to suggest an evolving story, a pattern of formative moments in the life of a poet who, born into a Liverpool seafaring family before the Second World War, grew up in the bombed back-streets of Bootle ... Progress is mapped from the emotional intensities of home in Bulwer Street ... towards university at Cambridge, then half-a-lifetime's teaching, mostly in higher education.[10]

Several of the poets in *Liverpool Accents* quote a phrase from Simpson's poem 'Bootle Streets' about the 'ocean-minded streets' adjoining the docks that were the cityscape of his upbringing. Crudely, these streets had to do for Simpson what the mountains did for Wordsworth; they awaken peculiarly fraught, mixed emotions of fascination, intrigue and fear, the sense of some great force that is neither wholly benign nor wholly understood. The Wordsworthian parallel could go further, for this poetic enterprise of sustained introspection and retrospection results in the kind of verse autobiography that we see in *The Prelude*. The key poem 'Making Arrangements' begins with this sense of streets as 'lines of force' whose pull cannot be wholly resisted, even by those whose path takes them to Oxbridge or the lecture theatre rather than across 'the thousand miles of furrowed brine/ of fragrant isles' ('Bootle Streets') which lead to ports all around the world ('Hobart, Valpo, Montevideo') and the engine rooms and crews' bars on freighters and passenger ships. 'Making Arrangements', then, constantly promises (or threatens) to say that 'geography is destiny': if the opening lines are true, then the poet/speaker, who never went to sea, must be marked and perhaps in some way broken by these forces, in respects other than the physical.

> Look at the map. The streets where I grew up
> move in a direction hard to resist,
> lines of force that drag down to grey docks,
> to where my father spent his strength.

Hence, even for the long-standing academic, the formative locale of these dockside streets lives on within. These streets are not comfortably in the past, away on the other side of the city and available as the *topoi* of nostalgic reverie, for the whole atmosphere is one of uncomfortable, half-understood complicity with the hardness and even brutality they engender. The poem continues:

> I am making these arrangements into meaning
> to re-inhabit after twenty years some places of
> myself – backyards full of ships and cranes,
> of hard-knock talk, and death – not just
> to mouth at ghosts, unless there's welcoming
> in such a courtesy; not merely exorcise:
> I'd like to talk at this late stage on equal terms,
> declare a kind of coming of age
> to those who have implanted death in me.

The phrase 'some places of/ myself' is striking, and implies that this is a kind of return to a primeval first locale; but unexpectedly, the 'lines of force' are still potent and choices made long ago demand to be rehearsed and justified all over again. For instance, the intransitive use of the verb 'drag' is curious, and suggests an omission:

> The streets drag down to the docks – to warehouses,
> dericks, pigeons, and hard men
> that I resisted twenty years ago
> by riding inland, choosing softer options
> they would say.

Here the phrase 'choosing softer options' sounds a note of guilt at the inevitable severance from that childhood background, and this note is a constant in work by all those poets whose trajectory includes social-class transition (Heaney and Tony Harrison are obvious poetic parallels). In Simpson it sounds most clearly in 'Latin Master', which is about an archetypal figure in such transitions – the schoolteacher who opens the way for the crossing of social boundaries by general encouragement, or by lending books, or merely by suggesting books to read. Thus the speaker becomes a spy at home, or a class traitor, or a turncoat (to use the emotive inner language used in the poem itself): 'His Latin verbs put me to work/ inside the fort,/ made turncoat of me in the end'. Hence, gradually the teacher's introduction of Bach or Brahms 'lost us our purchase on the things of home,/ made traitors of us to our kind'. So the anti-localising force of education counters and defeats the local force, the oceanward drag of the streets: 'he altered all our history,/ until the sea/ seemed to loose its dragging power/ and we learnt to hate our dockland streets/ and know ourselves barbarian'. The resulting transpersonal subjectivity envisages a peculiar intimacy between normally discrete entities – person and place, present and past, father and son – as if the speaker is somehow beginning to doubt the very notion of individuality, even though one might suppose that an increasingly sure sense of the self and a confident possession of its prerogative of existential self-improvement would be one of the products of the life trajectory this personal *Prelude* describes. At one level this intergenerational subjectivity has a simple physical counterpart, for the line 'those who have implanted death in me' refers to the speaker's recognition of a hereditary illness, suggested more explicitly in 'Once', which asserts that 'the dead/ are too expensively alive/ in the bone, the membrane,/ the organ out of tune'.

The notion of the street as a portion of the self, locus of the transpersonal self which collates father and son, place and person and past and present, recurs in 'Blossom Street'. This ancestral place is part of his father's life, and 'From here his ruined boyhood comes/ spilling into what I have become./ This is where the sea begins its mutterings.' The mutterings, presumably, arc within the speaker and are in the main accusatory. The accusation is implicit here but explicit in 'Home from Home', where it receives its starkest and most memorable expression:

> Education, also, exalted and betrayed.
> I was the sailor's son who never put to sea.
> I left the city like
> the Cunard liners and returned
> to find their red and black
> familiar funnels gone from gaps
> between the houses where I'd lived.

One of the most interesting things about poems such as this is their inherent assumption of a kind of benign integrity embodied within these streets, in spite of the embitterment and family cruelty that they also engender, which Simpson is keen to depict; any merely nostalgic or elegiac rendition of the past is explicitly disowned. Betrayed and seduced by education, the scholarship boy turns away from his upbringing and in doing so loses some vital self, so that in middle age the *revenant* comes back to these scenes from the past seeking something vital that is buried there but which, by his and its very nature, he can never find, so that the search itself merely increases his sense of self-disdain for the act of abandonment. In the James Bulger case these 'Bootle dockland streets' were the subject of very different speculation; it was suggested that the very nature of the terrain – now converted to anonymous high-rise blocks, vast, impersonal shopping malls and fast urban freeways – somehow generated the unfeeling sensibility which contributed to the crime, or caused ordinary people to fail to notice a small child's seemingly obvious distress.

The question remains: Which world is given in return for the one which is lost? The answer, in part, is that in place of Liverpool the poet receives England, for it is Vaughan Williams's *Lark Ascending* which (in the poem of that name) Simpson imagines being played at his own wake, 'when everyone's half-canned/ on Scotch and almost out/ of dissolute affection', and it's difficult to imagine anything more likely to harden the sneer in the seagull eyes or draw the lace curtains more tightly shut. For the spirit (his own) which passes to the skies with the music is 'something perhaps/ (was this what Brooke naively meant?) embarrassingly English'. This claim to Englishness is extremely unusual in the Liverpool setting – bizarre, even, in the context of a city whose claimed affiliations are always with the US, Ireland or some other territory, but never with its own regional environment. While the father's voyages always led in the end to 'approaching land,/ rope to bollard, feet again on stone' ('Seagulls'), the son's departure was like that of 'the last/ Cunarder facing the horizon' ('The Other Side of the Street') which never saw harbour again. The educated turncoat can never know home and landfall again, even in the painful sense of home expressed in R. S. Thomas's poignant line 'You are home. Come in and endure it.' He is now, as Thomas put it, exiled in his own country.[11]

This mention of Thomas offers a transition to the work of Deryn Rees-Jones, who is Anglo-Welsh. Her prefatory statement in *Liverpool Accents* points to the peripheral status of Liverpool in her work, for she writes that 'Only one of the poems in my first book, *The Memory Tray*, refers specifically to a Liverpool geography, but then very few of my poems incorporate real places'. The poem in question, called 'Soap', explores the Liverpool of popular representation ('there are a lot of clichés about Liverpool that I hate – which is what prompted the poem "Soap"'), and against these one-dimensional images she places a counter-balancing personal image of the city, viewing it as a series of faultlines where the tectonic plates of several different cultures meet and overlap, with resulting tensions and frictions ('I value being part of a city that contains such a variety of people, that is a place where Wales, and Ireland, and the North meet'). Though, of course, the notion of the city's cultural mix is a common one – almost a cliché itself, in fact – the emphasis on Liverpool as part of a nexus of interconnections is an unusual one. More often, its uniqueness is stressed, that sense of its being a kind of psychological island which (in John Kerrigan's words in the introduction to *Liverpool Accents*) is 'an international city which was cut off from its hinterland … somewhere distinctive yet oddly nowhere' and with an 'air of embattled alienation' (p. 3). The first of the three sections of Rees-Jones's *The Memory Tray* focuses strongly on the figure of her maternal grandmother (to whom the volume is jointly dedicated), and the introduction to her section of *Liverpool Accents* also seems to turn on this figure in a way that closely identifies her with the city itself ('She used to work as a secretary at the Liverpool Philharmonic in the 1930s'). The details cited also link her closely to Rees-Jones's notion of the city as containing 'such a variety of people': 'At one time she had a Chinese boyfriend called Willie Chung (a daring alliance in those days, I imagine). Later she fell in love with a Scottish cabinet maker called Alec.' Though only one of her own poems, as already indicated, 'refers specifically to a Liverpool geography', she ends the brief introduction with a moving comment that interestingly introduces street geography of the Matt Simpson kind, again evoking the idea of an urban landscape that has as much personal significance to the perceiving and growing subject as Wordsworthian mountains, and holds and forms the imagination and the emotions just as tightly:

> Ten years ago, when my grandmother was being taken to hospital for the final time, she asked the ambulance driver to do her a tour of the city so she could see it all before she died. I often think of that and wonder which route they took, and whether she saw the places that she wanted to. Sometimes I try to imagine it. And hope that she was satisfied. (p. 117)

Yet it is difficult at first in these poems to *see* the city (though it is heard and felt), for they are very much poems of interiors, so that the external geography of social space is merely something whose presence might be inferred in an opening like 'It might be any winter, any furnished room – / a table with a tablecloth, a pot-plant in a pot' ('The Chair'); or 'Being girls, we thought it best to love the Greeks/ sedately taught us in an attic schoolroom' ('Loving the Greeks'). Alternatively, urban geography is the implied hostile or indifferent circumambience of the consecrated interior space that provides the setting for tender intimacies:

> A siren flashes blue and mute
> Like the moon on a bender,
> Staggering drunkenly around the room
> As still our bodies sympathise.
> > ('Interim')

Here the exterior enters threateningly into the privacy of the room, like a drunk from the streets who has blundered in by mistake. Indeed, more often, geography is internalised and made merely metaphorical: this is the world turned inside-out, a classic trope of the love poem (as in John Donne's 'one little room' that becomes 'an everywhere'). Hence, near the opening of 'Shadowplay' in the context of 'strange geographies of hurt':

You hold my head in your hands
As if it were a globe
Rocking me slowly
From side to side. As if love
Were a country, difficult to place.

In what follows the lover projects shadows of animal shapes onto the walls, and the space of the encounter is thus mimed as both macro (a globe, a country) and micro ('the blank walls of the familiar room'), but without the intervening dimension of the local exterior – the familiar streets, rather than the familiar room – which are precisely the dimension that the intensity of love seems to eliminate. The temporal dimension in the same genre of erotic poetry loses its middle in exactly the same way; lovers live in the now (micro) and are conscious of the brevity of human life in the context of eternity (macro), but eliminate the day-to-day – the intricate temporal geometry of meals, pastimes and daily work (Vaneigem's 'everyday' life, which cries out, usually in vain, for transformation). The internalised geography occludes the middle element; the lover is the person who 'taught me at seventeen/ To make myself a body map', and the room and the self float in a dislocated space without a hinterland, like the Liverpool evoked by several of the *Liverpool Accents* poets. 'Afterward' likewise remains firmly inside the room ('Here, in the darkness, I might be with you for the first time'), and the poems continue to operate within a scenario that is almost entirely interior, like the hermetically sealed-off interior spaces of the *film noir* genre in which passion and menace, once removed from the quotidian, become oddly aligned. The conventionally dangerous space beyond the consecrated interior is hinted at, again, in citing the window and the colour blue, as the environment gradually re-materialises in the post-erotic calm ('Later, in a moment of moonlight,/ We are ordinary again,/ Striped by the shadows of the blue venetian blind'). The moment is presented in a strikingly filmic way, since the seeing eye/seeing 'I' sees *both* of the people involved ('Our gleaming eyes are beacons'), whereas the homodiegetic persona would see only one pair of eyes.

The two final poems of the middle section of the book (the section which centres upon intimate, room-based poems of erotic *frisson*) both use explicit cinematic allusions, and complete a kind of progression that is rather like that of James Joyce's *Portrait of the Artist as a Young Man*; there is a gradual shift from the Part 1 material that centres on childhood memories to the room-based intimacy poems of Part 2, to an altogether more public kind of writing (using filmic and cultural referentia, for instance) in Part 3. Here, the poems contain public events and established cultural icons (Yeats's marriage in 'William and Georgie, 1917', *Star Trek* in 'Lovesong to Captain James T. Kirk', high art in 'Leonardo', mythology in 'Porphyria' and so on). In 'Connections' a chance encounter through a misdialled phone call evokes a kind of self-scrutiny from a personal and national perspective in response to a voice from the other side of the world that asks her whether she is English. She says she is, but uses the Welsh word for it ('Am I English? *Saesneg*, I explain'). Likewise, her landscape is literally both English and Welsh, but the Welsh mountain is barely remembered, and the Welsh word for it mispronounced ('I have stars, I say, English stars, A Welsh mountain I can/ Just remember – *mynydd* – a word I can't pronounce too well').[12] So the circumambient cultural geography is bewildering, complex and far from reassuring, but this time the speaker's habit of turning inwards to the familiar room boundaries of personal space also fails to reassure:

> In this room
> I have newspapers
> Three days old. A vase of dying flowers. The radio.
> I have the voices of the politicians. Books. An atlas
> I can't find either of us on.

Here again, then, the middle ground between the microscape of the room and the global macroscape that contains the two callers is curiously absent. The landscape of arctic wilderness around the distant caller is placed with metonymic precision ('the snow has never been so thick,/ Caking her lonely wooden house./ The gutters spill water/ the colour of flour'). Yet the corresponding urban midscape around the speaker at the other end of the phone is conspicuously absent, even though the infrastructure that allows its superstructure expression – newspapers, radio, politics, books – is directly mentioned. Such things are precisely what make the wilderness described in the first half of the poem no longer that, even though (the city-bound speaker thrillingly imagines) you might hear from the distant fir woods 'The comforting roar of the hoarse brown bear'.

I will turn finally to Robert Hampson's *Seaport*, a work very different in character and provenance from all the material considered so far. *Seaport* is in four parts, published as a 46-page A4-sized book by Hampson's own Pushtika Press, in what is described as an 'interim edition' since

Part 4 is incomplete, being represented by just two fragments included as an appendix. The work is part of the avant-garde of contemporary British poetry – an old-fashioned term, but one quite frequently used to designate work that is Modernist in technique, with provenances and allegiances that include (on the American side) Ezra Pound, Charles Olson, William Carlos Williams, the 'New York' poets, the Objectivists, the 'LANGUAGE' poets, and (to some extent) John Ashbery; and (on the British side) Basil Bunting, J. H. Prynne, Roy Fisher, Allen Fisher and Eric Mottram. Poets working within this sphere have tended to shun conventional outlets and have set up a wide network of alternative literary sociology with its own bookshops, journals, presses, poetry events and conferences.[13]

Seaport makes extensive use of incorporated data of various kinds, including literary sources such as Joseph Conrad's sea novels; Herman Melville's *Redburn* (1849) (which, of course, itself uses the same model and incorporates extensive documentary material on the port of Liverpool in the middle of the nineteenth century); the Liverpool material in Washington Irving's *Sketchbook* (1819–20); Daniel Defoe's account of Liverpool in *A Tour through the Whole Island* (1724–26); letter and diary comments from Nathaniel Hawthorne written during his period as American Consul in Liverpool; and so on. These are not just brief allusions lifted out of context and pasted in, as in *The Waste Land*, but identified quotations in the manner of Pound's later *Cantos*. A further strand of data takes in material from historical accounts of the growth and development of the port, the history of race relations in the city, newspaper accounts of local events and local guidebooks. The verse that links or incorporates this material is spare and taut, avoiding any kind of lexical or imagistic embellishment, and apparently acting simply as a denotative seeing eye.

However, although the style and register seem at first to be fairly homogeneous throughout, there are in fact four clear stages that indicate different degrees of intervention in the adopted material. I will focus on this technical aspect of the poem, since in my experience the most frequent demand made of the explicator of this kind of writing is for a demonstration (or laying bare) of the procedural or structural principles on which it is organised. The first stage, then, is that of minimal intervention; the poet does a simple cut-and-paste job from the sources, and the passages used are set on the page as prose with label identifiers, like quotations in an academic essay. For instance, page 9 displays a series of quotations from Quentin Hughes's book *Seaport* (1964) and from Defoe. These might be taken as a series of epigraphs, but they are not placed at the start of the work, or even the start of the section, so that the effect is to deconstruct the distinction between the textual and the paratextual (in Genette's sense; that is, boundary-marking features such as titles, subtitles, epigraphs, and so on). Implicitly, this raises fundamental issues about where things begin and end. Did the notorious murder of Charles Wooton by a white mob in Liverpool in 1919 (see Part 4 of the poem) begin with Liverpool's involvement with the slave trade? Did the arrest of a 17-year-old black youth for dropping a chip-paper in Granby Street, Liverpool, in July 1981 (also in Part 4) have its genesis at the same time? And has it ended yet?

The second stage involves slightly more intervention with the source material; sentences are selected and taken out, rather than text being lifted in paragraph-sized blocks. They are then isolated into significant phrase-units and arranged on the page, so that it begins to look like, say, the notes that a lecturer might make in preparing to speak on a topic. For instance, this is the start of page 16 (I have numbered the pages through, calling the title page page 1):

> between 1846
> and 1855
>   nearly three million people emigrated from Britain
>
> the majority   from Ireland to North America
>   by way of Liverpool.
> The famine of 1846
>   (more fully reported in Canada
>   than in the British press)
> was followed by typhus in 1847

The third stage takes the source material into a minimalist poetic register, whereby words and brief phrases on a carefully sculpted page are made to resonate strongly because of the unusual spacing and grouping. Words are isolated by space markers of various sizes, indicating reading pace, degrees of emphasis and units of breath; the page is composed as a spatial entity, not just as a linear sequence, usually with minimal punctuation and capitalisation. These procedures are part of a clear line of development running from William Carlos Williams's 'variable foot', Pound's 'ideogrammatic method', Olson's 'Projective Verse' and Eric Mottram's 'mosaic' style. The opening page, for instance, is 'perch rock' (named after the New Brighton fort that is the innermost landmark for ships approaching the port of Liverpool):

> ships   move in
> > from the bay
> close to the flat   coastline of Crosby
> > into the narrows
>
> perch rock   stands
> > to starboard
> the close
> > vestibular   landline
> > > runs
> > > > from   the point blocks
> > > > > of flats
> to the graceful lines
> > of dark-brick
> > terraced houses.

In this instance the technique has been to draw out latent poetic qualities from prose sources by editing and re-spacing the material, so again the process of composition is deliberately pared down and the scope for poetic 'flights' is crafted out, just as a Modernist building presents a plain surface that can be part of an overall compositional massing, but is not allowed to provide a frame for decorative embellishments. All the same, the effect is now distinctly poetic, whereas the effect in the first two stages was distinctly prose-like.

Finally, in the fourth stage the poetic effect is heightened further, to such an extent that the material might be mistaken for personal observation. This is from Part 4, 'The Leaving of Liverpool', which concerns the 1960s cultural boom period, and page 30 is headed 'you can't dance to art (Merseybeat 1962–64)' and reads complete:

> a suburban
> music shop
> youth in a
> collarless
> jacket
> fingers the
> chord

A minor
on guitar
cuban-heeled
boot rests on
tiny amp
Vox AC30
(amp &
speaker
combined)
you could
carry it
yourself

the simplicity.

Here the period is marked by sharp metonymic details such as the collarless jacket, the Cuban heels and the now quaintly modest-seeming audio equipment; the poem has an iconographic quality whereby its slim line suggests, perhaps, the neck of the guitar, or the slimness of the youth himself. Likewise, its ultra-cool tone makes no attempt to impress us with emotive, evocative, sensitive or ingenious diction – the poem simply isn't in that sort of game at all – and hence mirrors the assured self-possession of the guitarist who will use his minimal resources (the three-chord trick, so called) to produce magical effects. *Seaport*, then, offers another version of the hard lyric, providing a large-scale vehicle of surprising flexibility that can accommodate the overtly political, the archival-historical, and radically pared down versions of poetry's more familiar affective modes.

I have polarised the 1960s and the 1990s work pretty starkly throughout. A different essay could easily have been written that would emphasise throw-backs, anticipations and continuities between the Liverpool poetry of the two periods (providing a proleptic view of the 1960s juxtaposed with an analeptic view of the 1990s). McGough and Patten are major writers and performers still, as was Henri right up until his recent death, and their work has, of course, not remained fossilised in the long-ago moment of 1965 when Liverpool was the centre of human consciousness. Thus Henri appears in the 1990s *Liverpool Accents* anthology, and '1990s' poet Matt Simpson actually belongs to the same generation. The benign, pastoral city of the 1960s produced a body of work whose tone never dwindled to a narrowly provincial monologia, even while it celebrated its vigorous loco-specificity. In the 1990s, as the city emerged from the traumatising 1980s, it has produced a much more troubled and troubling kind of writing. It has, in both senses, re-registered its poetic claims. What links the poets of the two decades is their realisation that poetry can be written (in Patten's phrase) 'Right there among the Woodbines and Guinness stains', that 'this city with winds and grass blowing through' is potentially the site of poetry. This seems elementary, but realising it is always a breakthrough, for the rural, neo-Georgian carapace of poetry has proved amazingly resistant to change. The Oxford University Press poetry list debacle showed, I think, that poetry in general cannot afford to babble of green fields forever. In the end, I believe, only the hard urban lyric, like that of these Liverpool poets, will be able to rescue it from commercial and academic oblivion.

Notes

1 See the many reports of this event in the British national press in late 1998 and early 1999, such as 'Minister attacks dons as "barbaric"', *Independent*, 4 February 1999.

2 The book, which revealed for the first time Hughes's responses to his relationship with Sylvia Plath and its aftermath and was published just before his death, won the Whitbread Poetry Prize, the Whitbread Book of the Year Award and the T. S. Eliot Memorial Prize.

3 *Contemporary British Poetry and the City*, Manchester, Manchester University Press, 2000.

4 Edward Lucie-Smith, *The Liverpool Scene*, London, Donald Carroll, 1967, p. 15.

5 Jonathan Raban, *The Society of the Poem*, London, Harrap, 1971.

6 Raoul Vaniegem, *The Revolution of Everyday Life*, trans. Donald Nicholson-Smith, Seattle, Left Bank, 1983; the quotation is from Chapter 20, 'Creativity, Spontaneity and Poetry'.

7 *Against Interpretation and Other Essays*, London, Deutsch, 1987 (1966).

8 Edited by Peter Robinson and published by Liverpool University Press in 1996.

9 Robert Hampson, *Seaport*, Woking, Pushtika Press, 1995.

10 Matt Simpson, *An Elegy for the Galosherman: New and Selected Poems*, Newcastle-upon-Tyne, Bloodaxe, 1990, p. 128.

11 These phrases occur in 'The Lost', one of the poems in Thomas's *No Truce with the Furies* (Bloodaxe, 1995): 'We are exiles within/ our own country/ "Show us",/ we supplicate, "the way home". "But you are home. Come in/ and endure it."'

12 Rees-Jones is one of the younger Welsh poets praised by Ian Gregson in a brief and controversial article in *New Welsh Review* (No. 27, winter 1994, pp. 22–23) entitled 'An Exhausted Tradition', which attacked younger Welsh poets for their adherence to the 'exhausted tradition' represented, says Gregson, by R. S. Thomas and Seamus Heaney, whom he sees as 'products of comparatively static rural cultures whose preoccupations are largely irrelevant to anyone brought up with television'. Gregson sees her as representative of fractured postmodern multiple identities, exploring 'mixed Welsh and English ancestry alongside other issues – especially those of gender and the extent to which identity is destabilized by sexual desire'. The article was followed up with heated correspondence in subsequent issues of the journal.

13 For general accounts of this area of activity see such books as Robert Hampson and Peter Barry (eds), *New British Poetries*, Manchester, Manchester University Press, 1993; Clive Bush, *Out of Dissent: Five Contemporary British Poets*, London, Talus, 1997; and Richard Caddell and Peter Quartermain, *Other British and Irish Poetry Since 1970*, Middletown, CT, Wesleyan University Press, 1998.

REFLECTIONS ON THE CRAFT

2

Liverpool Peasant

Michael Murphy

for Judith Palmer

Let me retrace my steps.
Louis Aragon, Paris Peasant

I was brought up in one of Liverpool's many quiet suburbs. Most of the area's housing had been built after the Second World War. There was a smattering of schools and small shops, but no local cinema. The only public spaces were churches or pubs. It seemed designed for a certain kind of private life, one that focused on the domestic. My mum was an auxiliary nurse in Oxford Street Maternity Hospital; my dad painted the green-and-cream livery on Merseyside's buses. He also stencilled the zebra stripes onto a bus advertising Knowsley Safari Park and painted the sunflower-yellow railway carriage still on exhibit in the basement of Liverpool Museum. His grandfather had migrated from Wexford. Her family were Protestants from Orange Dingle. In marrying my father, she had converted to Catholicism in order not to offend the religious mores of the late 1950s. They were and remain a quiet, respected, generous and well-loved couple. It has taken me 30-odd years to recognise and admire these qualities.

We had a succession of small cars. The first that I remember was a pale-blue Morris Minor, a kind of soap bubble on wheels. Perhaps my earliest memory is attached to this car: I am sitting in the shady back seat and being handed a warm bundle through the open door. My sister. This locates my first recollected stirrings of consciousness at two-and-a-half years. There may be earlier ones: watching a metallic red fire engine turn circles on the living-room carpet while its lights flashed blue against the blue sky beyond the window; being bathed in a tub in front of a coal fire. Unlike the incident in the Morris Minor these images don't attach themselves to a precise date. As such they exist outside time.

It always surprises me that memory allows us to see ourselves objectively. For example, I see the child playing with the fire engine as though the adult me were standing in the room and watching him from behind. As Milan Kundera comments in *Immortality*, memory allows us to view ourselves not as cinema but as snapshot. In hindsight, life becomes a series of fragmentary pages in an album. And not always arranged in their true order.

The significance of my sister's arrival was heightened by the fact that both she and I were adopted. Like everyone, adoptive children want an answer to the question 'Where do I come from?' In a sense, the answer is the same for us all. Courtesy of *Encarta* and the laptop on which I'm writing this, I can tap in 'conception' and show my quizzical six-year-old nephew moving footage of all our biological origins: sperm dashing towards the red tape of the egg's circumference; a swarm of question marks geared to dancing on the head of a pin. But this isn't what the adopted child means. Or not principally. At two-and-a-half, I knew I didn't come from my mother's tummy. But back there in the Morris Minor I was given some kind of reference point by which to orientate myself. Collecting my sister, I was suddenly a participant – a character, even – in the same story my parents had told me: *Once upon a time we went to a large white house. In that house there was a room full of pink and blue cots. In each cot there was a baby. What we had to do was choose just one of those babies...* Growing up, these were the only facts I had. It's just that not all of them were true.

For a long time my sister and I were not allowed to play out in the street on a Sunday. Instead, we had to limit our simmering rivalries to the flowerbedded confines of the back garden. At the time, I thought this was some form of Catholic observance: no breakfast before mass, a glass of water on returning to the house after Communion, and then an afternoon of trying not to kick the ball through next door's greenhouse windows. Perhaps in part it was. Another reason is the simple fact that my dad worked overtime most nights of the week. His Saturdays were devoted to fishing. Sunday, then, was the only day our parents enjoyed together with their children.

If this was my private life, I had another existence outside the home. As children we – my friends and myself – had the kind of elbow-room of which I suspect most children and young parents in today's city can barely conceive. At the top of our road (named after a British governor of India) was a park. Nearby was a large girls' secondary school with playing fields and tennis courts backing onto a disused, overgrown railway. If we exercised our bodies on the hockey fields, the railway, with its dark tunnels and eerie silences, stimulated our imaginations. To be dared to walk alone through one of those tunnels was to confront every fear we had ever had instilled into us.

As with most children, we were fiercely territorial. A friend whose parents up and moved to a house barely 20 minutes' walk away was baffled to discover he now lived in Knowsley. We teased him about becoming a 'woollyback' – the Liverpudlian equivalent of a hick, a country cousin. Some kind of border had been erected between us. It's not that we saw that much less of him, just that he was no longer a part of the same talismanic world of swapping football cards at street corners, playing hide-and-seek in the grainy half-light of dusk, or flicking through a cache of 'dirty' pictures found stuffed into a neighbour's hedge. For a while these were the coordinates of our lives. Then they would shift, expanding and contracting like our own thickening bodies.

I suspect that the childhood I'm describing was the norm for those of us lucky enough to grow up during the relatively liberal 1970s. And in doing so, in mapping the kinds of liberties and imaginative spaces we enjoyed, I find that I am challenging my own assumptions about the kinds of early experiences necessary to a writer or any other kind of artist. By my late teens I was deeply resentful of my upbringing and environment. There were no books in the house. The only pictures we had were photographs of my sister and I as children. I had been alienated by a secondary education marked by the intellectual and spiritual cowardice of teachers in thrall to the Jesuit priests who ran the joint. Only when I came to read Dickens did I realise that my schooling was a brutal anachronism. Things changed, however, even during my time. During my last year in the sixth form, the school lost its grammar status. The upshot was that one priest ran away and got married, and the headmaster had a nervous breakdown. Dotheboys Hall had to adjust to becoming Dotheboys High. Corporal punishment and the 11-plus went out the same third-floor window from which I had once seen a classmate being dangled.

Almost my last memory of school is of being at a party and watching another student passionately defending the merits of Shelley as a poet. A teacher was obviously disagreeing with the boy, who unexpectedly burst into tears. I had never seen another pupil cry – or only when thwacked with a strip of whalebone-reinforced leather. I had no real idea who Shelley was; I'd read precious little poetry. I only knew that he must be important if this boy, who I knew was captain of the rugby team, could let his feelings slip so publicly.

Armed with a mediocre academic record and a comprehensive know-ledge of 1960s psychedelic pop, I was given a job as a claims and insurance clerk with the same bus company for which my dad had worked since the age of 16. When I think about the books I read at this time – the only years during which I've had to wear a tie as a matter of habit – each is clearly associated in my mind with a particular place: *Ulysses* I began in my doctor's surgery; *The Rainbow* on the H5 bus stuck in torrential rain on Picton Road; Kafka I bought in the first Dillons on Lord Street; *The Waste Land* I read, nonplussed but hypnotised by the syncopated jazz rhythms, propped up behind a stack of insurance files one slow Friday afternoon at the office; and *The Brothers Karamazov* taught me the dangerous truth that novels could become substitutes for life.

The writer who meant most to me, then as now, was Proust. Nine months it took me to plough through the Penguin three-volume edition of *À la recherche du temps perdu* that I carried with me everywhere like Mao's *Little Red Book*. I read him on buses, over tea breaks at work, in the pub, on the beach, and blissfully snowbound at a week's residential course in management and leadership skills in North Yorkshire. I finally finished him one night under swathes of blankets in the first of a succession of damp flats out towards the sea in Formby. Gradually, Proust's Paris began to take on a reality that was synonymous with my own journeys to and from work, to the theatre, to the Bluecoat cinema and on my first trips abroad. This was also when I began writing. Or, more accurately, began deferring writing. As I read and assimilated different writers' voices, so I wrote snatches of poems and filled notebooks with half-finished stories. I plotted novels as intricate as *Ulysses*, based on my own chaotic love-life and aesthetic fumblings, but somehow nothing ever got finished. Discipline only entered my life when, as an undergraduate, I started writing oblique Pirandelloesque dramas and directing plays by Samuel Beckett and Howard Barker.

Looking back, it is interesting to see just how much I mis-read Proust. As with Joyce's *A Portrait of the Artist as a Young Man*, I saw only what I thought I had in common with Stephen and Marcel: the desire to re-make myself as a writer. I was in awe of Stephen's intellect and Marcel's sensibility. What I missed, however, were those elements of the novels that satirised both central characters and their half-baked aesthetics, their snobbery and naivety. Of course I missed those things. One reason both authors have such a powerful hold over us is that they have the knack of tricking the reader into believing that s/he is not passively

reading a book but actively *writing* it. In other words, they are so won-
derfully accurate about the processes of being a writer that, like the
lotus flowers encountered by Odysseus, they take away any desire to
begin the hard work of writing oneself.

It seems to me that it is fatal to overdetermine the creative process. The
imaginative spaces out of which we create have to be allowed to main-
tain a certain residual mystery. In other words they have to keep us
guessing, like a potential lover. Catching sight of an object out the
corner of one's eye means that the exact nature of the object remains
fluid, indeterminate. For as long as it remains so the imagination can
give it any texture, shape or colour it wants. It can be a desk lamp, or it
can be a heron stalking suburban fishponds. The same is true when, as
in this essay, a writer is trying to explain something of his own imagi-
native and verbal processes. As anyone who has ever written a letter
knows, there is no simple equation between our experiences and desires
and how we subsequently fit them to speech. It is all too easy to lie to
the other person; it is even easier to deceive ourselves.

Having said this, some of my early experiences in relation to growing
up in Liverpool have affected the way I respond to and shape language.
The vernacular here is a jumble of influences – Irish, Scots, Welsh, North
American, Caribbean and Scandinavian. Sentences jink off at odd tan-
gents, tricking us into saying things we couldn't have meant if we tried,
and this has affected the city's writers. Matt Simpson for one has
repeatedly mined this essentially tragi-comic aspect of the dialect. I
wonder if it isn't for similar reasons that Deryn Rees-Jones's poetry is
strongly influenced by surrealism. This, in part, is where the city's sub-
versive energies are stored. Hardly surprising, then, if over time the lan-
guage we have to describe the world begins to determine the very ways
in which we see it.

My writing is rarely driven by anything specifically Liverpudlian.
Having said that, I can still find some connections between the idiom
of this place and the structures of my work. Perhaps I can give an
example.

Elsewhere

Do you remember burying the thrush
we found laid out stiff on the cinder track
beside the railway; perfect as a mammoth,

swaddled in a coat of soil and permafrost,
how you wrapped him in a Kleenex
among the broken pots, split canes and bulbs
sprouting in the loamy darkness
under your dad's shed?
                    All night,
at opposite ends of the city, we waited
to see if – if – feathers, beak and all the
intricately coiled stuff

had, with morning, ascended.

A kind of disappointed sonnet, the poem (like Scouse) is a mish-mash of influences and memories (not all of them my own), significant places, and, I suppose, aspects of the fundamental Christian mystery.

The bird in the poem is real enough. Only I didn't find it near a disused railway. I found it in a plastic carrier bag (the bag, by the way, crops up in another poem, 'Heimat', though there it is stuffed with fresh mint and wild garlic) lobbed over a fence near some trees. Thinking about it, I guess that this was the first dead thing I'd ever seen. Its eyes – small black inky rounds – weren't closed and the mottled breast struck me as exceptionally beautiful and vulnerable. I also knew that thrushes were migratory, and that this one was going nowhere. Everything else about the poem is a fiction. This isn't to say that the original experience, what we might – wrongly, I believe – call 'the truth', is diminished. What I wanted to do, what I try to do in all my writing, was to take a biographical event and re-orientate myself within it, finding a significance I may have missed at the time.

Susan Sontag has written that 'Reminiscences of self are reminiscences of a place, and how [the writer] positions himself in it, navigates around it.' As such, most first novels or collections of poetry tend to be autobiographical. After all, our own lives are the material that lies closest to hand. It is usually only later that the writer begins to move from the shallow waters of his or her own experience into the deeper currents of language itself. Joyce is an obvious example. In many ways my first collection of poems does precisely this, while pretending to be doing something else.

In 1997 I was given a small bursary that enabled me to travel and write. I had visited Budapest twice before and wanted an excuse to return. I contacted friends in the city and organised a three-week stay.

When I returned to Liverpool I had the basis of *After Attila* – 30-odd translations of the Hungarian poet Attila József, plus a series of poems of my own recording some of my encounters with the city. When I showed some of the József fragments to John Lucas, the editor of Nottingham's Shoestring Press, he wrote back to ask if there were enough for a pamphlet. This gave me the confidence to return to and rework a number of the poems, a batch of which I sent to Robert Minhinnick at *Poetry Wales*.

The process of writing what became *After Attila* changed not only how I wrote but, equally important, how I thought of myself as a writer. I cannot call myself a poet. My body of work doesn't yet merit it. What this first collection gave me, however, was a sense of having to write not sporadically but of needing to persist in mining a certain coherence of experience, language and style. In other words, to begin to find a voice. It also allowed me to set myself a challenge. The translations needed to be up to the mark or I would be letting József down; my own Budapest poems had to be of a certain quality or they would pale in comparison to József's muscularity. Whether I succeeded is for others to say. But in my own mind those poems are now a kind of benchmark on which I can't go back.

Liverpool is where I live and work. As in 'Elsewhere', it crops up in my poems in fragments, as a discontinuous presence among other cities. When, in 'The Last European', I wanted to write about Walter Benjamin, it was Liverpool – its cobble-stoned back alleys, the plague of bloody pigeons, the view of the broody Welsh hills – that I used as a model. It is as a European writer that I would want to define myself.

For me as for countless people in this city's not uncomplicated past and present, Liverpool is a place of arrivals and departures. Built by a largely migrant or immigrant population, the city feels unstable under my feet, as if wanting to throw off its moorings and slide out along the Mersey to drift free on the warm tides of the Gulf Stream. Or perhaps I'm giving in to my own feelings of unsettlement.

Four years ago I traced my birth mother to Dublin where she lives not five minutes' walk from the Martello Tower, Joyce's *omphalos*. Since our first meeting under the statue of John Middleton, the 'Childe of Hale', she has been able to show me the people and places from whom and where I came. I have written about these things, usually indirectly. Like Einstein, I'm more interested in seeing the back than the front of my head. I now have an Irish passport, but I can't say that I am Irish. My father, mom tells me, was from West Virginia. I feel lost in England; it's a matter of some essential gears or rhythms just not meshing. Like Elizabeth Bishop's Crusoe, 'my poor island's still/ un-rediscovered, un-renamable./ None of the books has ever got it right.' Perhaps this is how those Jews felt who, fleeing the pogroms of Eastern Europe for a new life in the US, were hoodwinked into believing that the Liverpool sky-line was New York.

'Not to find one's way about in a city is of little interest,' Benjamin wrote. 'But to lose one's way in a city, as one loses one's way in a forest, requires practice.' Following Rimbaud, Benjamin would have agreed that 'Life is elsewhere'. For the writer it is a matter of following this 'elsewhere' as it teems through the currents of language, as it manifests itself in the random daily occurrences of life. Partly this is a matter of simply casting oneself adrift, partly a case of catching hold of any drift-wood that happens to float past.

Screen Memories

The Kiss

Deryn Rees-Jones

Should we have stayed at home,
wherever that may be?
                    Elizabeth Bishop[1]

My childhood is preserved as a nation's history,
My favourite fairy tales the shells
Leased by the hermit crab.
                    Medbh McGuckian[2]

Like Freud's 'screen memories' which mask the actual traumatic events
of childhood – what Adam Phillips calls 'a waking dream of the past'–
the poem has a wonderful capacity to transform experience or make
something new of it, but also to disguise it. Sometimes this happens
consciously; sometimes it comes about simply through the process of
writing. Curiously, it isn't necessarily the most important feelings or
memories that make themselves available as poems. The 'tell it slant'
capacity of the poem, which allows the writer to be surprised, is one of
the things I enjoy most about writing: memories creep up and are
transformed, and become a way of not only knowing the self but of
rethinking one's own position in the world.

The process of remembering and forgetting one's own history and
personal mythology does, of course, become foregrounded and encoded
in the writing of the poem. Yet the question of my own relation to the
geography of the city in which I was born and lived for 18 years, and
have now returned to, is an interesting and difficult one. I rarely write
about known places, let alone my home city. Paradoxically, it is perhaps
exactly this denial of named geographies in my work that creates a
space out of which to write.

Two poets who are important to me as both a reader and a writer, and
who address the relationship with geography, are Elizabeth Bishop

(1911–79) and Fleur Adcock (born 1934). Both demonstrate the rela-
tionship of the self to the environment as a way of defining the place –
and sometimes placelessness – of the female observer. Bishop is the most
important poet to my work at the moment, though her influence is prob-
ably not immediately discernible. The epigraph to Bishop's *Geography III*,
taken from 'First Lessons in Geography', poses vital questions: 'What is
geography? What is a map?' This is immediately followed by 'In the Wait-
ing Room', a poem in which the realisation of female identity becomes
clear in a momentary layering of personal history (Aunt Consuelo's 'oh of
pain' in the dentist's chair) and an understanding of what it means to be
gendered female (the photograph of the black women with their 'horri-
fying breasts' in an issue of *National Geographic*). The locating of the self
physically for Bishop is a complex and ongoing preoccupation in her
work which overtakes the importance of a location in time, something
summed up in the early poem 'The Monument' which famously ends:
'More delicate than the historian's are the mapmaker's colours.'

   While Adcock's is a much less complex aesthetic than Bishop's, her
examination of her place as an outsider is keenly focused in a poem such
as 'A Surprise in the Peninsula', which tells the story of a woman, a
stranger to a village, who has a dead dog nailed to her door:

> On the flat surface of the pelt
> was branded the outline of the
> peninsula, singed in thick black
> strokes into the fur: a coarse map.
> The position of the town was
> marked by a bullet-hole; it went
> right through the wall. I placed my eye
> to it, and could see the dark trees
> outside the house, flecked with moonlight.[3]

Adcock was one of the first women poets I read, and I remember very
clearly taking out her *Selected Poems* from the central library in Liverpool.
Both these poets touch a nerve with me, perhaps because they say what
I do not feel able to say. The image of the woman who is a stranger to a
community peering out through the hole in a door, her eye filling the
hole on a map which in its turn places *her*, is a mesmerising and richly
metaphorical image.

   Placing oneself as a writer aesthetically, as well as identifying strongly
with a place, are often cited as key components in a poet's writing, as

well as an ability to stand apart from the region or nation that one writes about. Robert Crawford, in his book *Identifying Poets*, draws on Mikhail Bakhtin to examine the work of twentieth-century poets for whom the development of an identity 'with and for their own culture' arises 'through a fructifying engagement with another culture and literature'.[4] For both Bishop (the Canadian sent to the US who chose to live in Brazil) and Adcock (the New Zealander living in London) this is true. As a port, Liverpool is ideally situated to facilitate the cultural interchange of which Bakhtin talks – depressingly in Liverpool's case via a history of slavery and a colonial relationship with Ireland, and to a less extent Wales. However, in my case Liverpool remains a silent part of my writing self.

When I was beginning to write I was an undergraduate in North Wales, and a sense of my Welsh heritage became, in retrospect, a place from which to write and to remember my childhood. Assuming a space for myself as a Welsh writer became a part of my imaginative identity, a way of assuming an 'other self' who writes, leaving the self who now lives and works in Liverpool, the self who lived in London, in an unspoken part of my poetic consciousness. National identity is confused for me– as it probably is for many of my contemporaries – in my case because of my obviously Welsh name, my Welsh paternal grandparents and my periods of living in and out of Wales. The matter is further confused by a sense that I am culturally English: my upbringing and primary and secondary education enforced a certain kind of class-bound, reticent Englishness. It was only at the point when I left Liverpool that I started identifying it as a place to which I belonged – the Liverpool of the 1970s and 1980s in which I had grown up.

There are poets who write – or have written – very convincingly about Liverpool: Matt Simpson, Glyn Wright, Paul Farley, Jamie McKendrick and, of course, the Liverpool poets themselves (and it's surely of some relevance that they are all male), but it would be very painful indeed for me fix a poem to its locality: just the thought of mentioning Penny Lane, Mossley Hill or Hope Street brings me out in a cold sweat. Maybe paradoxically that's why I love Frank O'Hara's ambulatory 'I do this, I do that' poems, because they give you a mapped geography of New York. Joseph Clancy has produced a great pastiche of O'Hara in which he does for Bangor in North Wales what O'Hara does for New York, something I imitated in 'Blue', which mentions places that were some of my favourite haunts when I used to live in South London. On the whole, though, maybe I'm more able myself to think of geography in a poem as a psychic space. Certainly geography and the body seem to be closely linked in my mind. 'Soap' is my only published poem which talks about Liverpool as a 'real' place – and I wrote that living in London, a bit homesick for the Liverpool skyline and the river. I remember watching *Brookside* because it reminded me of home. The naming of Welsh places has become a bit of a joke in Welsh poetry written in English, a rather hackneyed badge of national identification. I mention Aberystwyth in the poem 'Half-Term', but then it represented more of a psychic space anyway. At the time of writing I hadn't been there, but because I felt close to my distant relative who did live there, I imagined the scenario of staying with her.

It was through my mother and my maternal grandmother that I got to know Liverpool, and through my maternal grandmother that I get a sense, however skewed, of my relationship to Liverpool history. She was born in Liverpool, left school at 14, was apprenticed as a secretary and ending up working in the Philharmonic Hall under the auspices of her boss, Mr Reilly. I remember promising her that when I grew up I would write down all the stories she would tell me about her pre-married life. The Liverpool of the 1930s and 1940s that she conjured up was one of glamorous evenings at the Philharmonic in the fragile silks and chiffons of evening dresses (some of which I later dressed up in), her fiancé Alec who died of TB, and her relatively late courtship and marriage to my Yorkshire grandfather. Reading about the local history of that time, I realise retrospectively what a selective tale I was told. There was no mention of the poverty that engulfed the city. Instead I heard of the visits of the Sarsaparilla man on a Friday evening; tram rides; my grandmother's Chinese boyfriend Willie Chung who inscribed the Angela Brazil novels she loved in perfect copperplate; and two key images that I associate clearly with a sense of the room in which she described them to me. These two memories have now been compressed into a single poem, 'The Kiss', probably one of the most accurate in terms of remembered truth I've ever tried to write.

So far this poem has gone through about five drafts; at each stage I've been surprised by what I remember, what I misremember and what I forget. Kitty was the name of my grandmother's cousin, and the story that she told me was of Kitty dying and being laid out in the parlour, while my grandmother still admired the long black hair she'd always envied. Almost certainly though her name wasn't Kitty O'Shea, a name originally associated with her because I'm told it was the name of Irish leader Charles Parnell's mistress. I realise now that I wonder about my grandmother's family, except for her mother, because we know very little about them; all I remember her telling me was that her grandparents on one side were Scottish and Irish, and that of her grandparents on the other side, one was Welsh and the other English. Knowing enough about my English and Welsh relatives, it seemed the poem was giving me a chance to explore what I didn't know about: the Scottish/Irish side. In the first draft the poem is titled 'Liverpool 1917'. It then becomes 'Liverpool 1916'; I was getting anxious about when my grandmother was actually 17 (she was born in 1907, but for some reason I remembered the date as 1900) and also what would have been happening in the First World War at that period. I didn't want to get it wrong, so rather than taking a chance or researching it, I transformed it into the metaphor that holds the whole poem together. Throughout the drafting process I found myself vacillating between wanting to give an obviously Liverpudlian setting, and trying to prevent the poem from being tied to a particular place. In the final draft the title has become 'The Kiss'. I realise now that the poem is a companion piece to an earlier poem which became the title of my second collection, 'Signs Round a Dead Body', but whereas that poem explores a male death that becomes developed thematically throughout the volume, 'The Kiss' reverts to the explorations of female identity – again through the images of the body – that I was preoccupied with in *The Memory Tray*.

The title opens the poem up, metaphorically, in a way a named location couldn't. I used to have Gustav Klimt's *The Kiss* on my wall as a teenager – the one Ferlingetti has a poem about in which the woman's lips are like tangerines. There's also a reference to the Judas kiss (my poems seem to be including more and more references to Christian iconography from my Anglican childhood now that I'm back in Liverpool). Apparently my grandmother was considering converting to Catholicism, something which her parents weren't very pleased about but which reluctantly they allowed her to do; and then she decided, almost at the last minute as it were, that being a High Anglican would suffice. When I stayed with her every weekend she would kneel at the bottom of the bed and say her prayers, and at church on Sundays she was the only member of the congregation to genuflect and cross herself. Her illness in the poem is also a remembered truth: I remember her telling me about falling ill with rheumatic fever which, she explained, 'turned her heart to jelly' (a phrase I edited out of the later version) and forced her to lie still in bed for weeks on end. The story of her father returning from the war is also 'true', as is the fact that he gave her what he thought would please her – a rosary he'd found on a dead soldier, which had been accompanied by a photo of the soldier's wife and child. Aunt Kitty was a cousin, as I remember, but on which side of the family I don't know. I remember my grandmother telling me as she plaited my hair how much admired were the young woman's long plaits, even as she lay in her coffin.

The poem is an important one in my own development, even if it never makes it to a third collection, which I suspect is likely. Telling too much of a truth, of a located history, seems to limit my ability to write a poem, closes down its own imaginative impetus. Perhaps only the final leaving of Liverpool would allow me to forget enough to write about the city, and find for it the 'strange half-truth' that a poem is.

The Kiss

My grandmother is quite the thing, with her shingled crop
and scarlet beret, her prayerbook waterlogged beside
the woollen swimsuit as she leaves the office where her fingers blur

to ride the tram through the dirty city; seagulls harassed
on cross currents above her, the Pier Head disappearing in a lurch,
as she turns away from the blackened river, planning the steps

of her conversion, swimming on those summer mornings
in the public baths: one hundred and fifty gunpowder lengths
of butterfly, of crawl. In a month or two rheumatic fever

will catapult her father from the Front to spend a night's
compassionate leave, his rifle propped against the bedroom door
as he threads a pillaged cedar rosary between her fingers

and she mutters the words of the Glorious Mysteries.
Her life depends on lying still. She recalls this now
a year has past, as she peers at her cousin in the shadowy parlour,

laid out in her coffin: red-mouthed, tubercular,
still-a-child Kitty; and places her lips on the frozen cheek;
one hand resting on the black plaited hair

bound at its ends by two brilliant bows
that settle like bluebirds at a waist so slender
she'd often boast a man, when they danced, could,
touching little finger on little finger, thumb on thumb,
meet his two strong hands around.

Notes

1   Elizabeth Bishop, 'Questions of Travel', *The Complete Poems*, London, Chatto and Windus, 1969, p. 107.

2   Medbh McGuckian, *The Flower Master*, Oxford, Oxford University Press, 1982, p. 21. Medbh McGuckian was very important to me as a writer early on. Her poem 'Slips' takes the footnotes from Freud's *The Psychopathology of Everyday Life* and transforms them almost word for word into a poem that comes to document the publicly unspoken parts of a woman's life.

3   Fleur Adcock, *Poems 1960–2000*, Newcastle-upon-Tyne, Bloodaxe, 2000, p. 38.

4   *Identifying Poets: Self and Territory in Twentieth-Century Poetry*, Edinburgh, Edinburgh University Press, 1993, p. 13.

A Poetry Residency in Tasmania
The Story behind Cutting the Clouds Towards[1]

Matt Simpson

In 1994 a letter came out of the Antipodean blue. It was from the Australian poet and organiser of the Tasmanian Poetry Festival, Tim Thorne, inviting me to take up a poetry residency at the Queen Victoria Museum and Art Gallery in Launceston, Tasmania. Launceston is Tasmania's second city (it has in effect the dimensions of a small market town); Hobart is its capital and the gateway to Antarctica.

There was more than just good fortune to it. Yes, it was like winning the lottery without knowing that someone had bought you a ticket. But it was also in a very special sense the place my psyche and poetry had always been heading for. It was the next stage in the kind of exploring I had for 20-odd years been doing in my writing. Suddenly there was the possibility of achieving – or partly achieving – some kind of resolution, making a kind of arrival. If you believed in destiny, you would think it was *meant,* predetermined. It was, to say the least, serendipitous.

In my earlier work – most notably in my first two collections, *Making Arrangements* (1982) and *An Elegy for the Galosherman* (1990) – I attempted to explore (as someone pulled away from it by education and by years of cinema- and church-going) what I will call 'Scouseness' and my own particular brand of it. Motivated by certain losses, regrets and a wish to come finally to terms, I tried making poems by interrogating my background and upbringing in a working-class family in Bootle, a family that had a strong tradition of seafaring and working with ships, which I was made in some ways to feel excluded from. It involved, among other things, an attempt to come to terms with how much of my father's character and language I had inherited; how much was me and how much him, and whether it would ever be possibile to reconcile these aspects of character.

There was always a feeling as I was growing up (sometimes spoken – 'there's your cousin John working on the trawlers!' – but it was mostly unspoken, yet always *there*) that I was betraying this seagoing tradition by heading towards a career in teaching and also indulging in that unmasculine pastime, writing poetry. OK, I had some experience of working at the Liverpool docks in my student vacations and, valuable as that experience was in helping me to understand my father's world (having been invalided out of seagoing after the Second World War, he was then working as a foreman rigger at Canada Dock), it was not the big world beyond the river mouth, beyond the horizon, that he had sailed to in his days as a merchant seaman.

The first poem in my second collection, 'Directions', puts the choice in this way:

> With a war to forget, we grew up
> on what was left of something, weeds
> on battered ground where houses once had stood:
>
> plantain tough as boots, irascible dock,
> dogged dandelion, and come-up-smiling rose-
> bay willow-herb among strewn bricks;
>
> streets of tar and cobble
> with dusty corner shops
> and lamp-posts you could swing on –
>
> ropes that smelt of creosote and ships:
> a centripetal spin into a vicious hug of iron,
> a centrifugal jerk to outer space.

Like most Scousers, my father was a bit of a hard-knock with a debunking, teasing humour and a fiercely protected soft centre. One thing he would tease me about was his visits to the Apple Isle, Tasmania. It was pretty obvious that he had romantic girl-in-port memories of the place, which only a gleam in his eye was ever going to betray. I put some of this into my poem 'The Call of the Genes':

> And you, dad, with rusty cut-water
> hauling out of Liverpool
> inside a riveted bucket of a thing,
>
> what tickled your fancy down-under there
> in the Roaring Forties?
> What apple blossom made your bosun's eye

twinkle thinking of Hobart? Who was
the girl-in-port you hoarded like pay slips?
Are there any more not home like me?

As a kid growing up in Liverpool, I thought all apples came from Tasmania: if you look on a map you might recognise an apple shape to the island, coloured green with brown mountains on some maps. How appropriate to the circumstances of my own life was this sentence from Shakespeare's *The Tempest*: 'I think he will carry this island home in his pocket and give it his son for an apple.' I just had to use it as an epigraph.

What I understood to be internal politicking in Tasmania over Seamus Heaney's intended trip down under that year meant that the residency had to be postponed until the following year, 1995. I took advantage of the time to freshen up and extend my knowledge of Australian literature. Because the trip was going to be my very first experience of flying, I was apprehensive about coping with 23 hours in the air. The thought of how many air miles my grandchildren had already clocked up helped to shame me into finally surrendering my flying virginity with a 40-minute flight from Liverpool to Dublin in the summer of 1994.

Then one day, in the remaindered-books shop in the Bluecoat Chambers, I found *The Penguin Anthology of Australian Women's Writing* edited by Dale Spender.[2] In it were extracts from the journal of an Englishwoman, Louisa Anne Meredith, who, having married her cousin, went to Australia in 1839. It was in particular her vivid and spirited account of the perilous ten-day journey she underwent from Sydney to Hobart in 1840 that enabled me to write a poem with which, as it were, I could chastise myself for apprehensions about flying. The fortitude shown by Louisa Anne Meredith put me to shame. She had undertaken a 12,000-mile sea voyage of several months to get to Australia (see her *Notes and Sketches of New South Wales*)[3] and now here was this bruising, nightmarish ten-day voyage to Hobart. I, in comparison, was going to sit in relative comfort in a jumbo jet and arrive there in just under a day. That poem (which I thought of simply as a one-off) was the start of what turned out to be a full-length collection eventually published by Liverpool University Press in 1998.

Louisa Anne was an artist and writer with a reputation established before she left England in 1839. The fact was that the more I read of her accounts the more fascinated I became and the more I had to admire her character. She was strong-minded, intrepid, full of exact observation and wicked humour – calling to mind many another strong-willed pioneering woman of the nineteenth century, the likes of Mary Kingsley or Florence Nightingale. By the time I finally took off from Manchester Airport on 25 September 1995, I had already written 14 poems about her – though, to be accurate, in some of them Louisa Anne and I exchange words and have conversations, so alive did she seem to me. These were published in Headland's Ariel series (note again *The Tempest* connection) under the title *To Tasmania with Mrs Meredith*. In them I felt able to enter more intimately than I had thought possible into something of the history of the Antipodes; I was also learning a great deal about their flora and fauna. It was a way in.

My one fear was that people in Tasmania might think that I was patronising them, appropriating one of their worthies and parading before them something they already knew. In the event I was relieved to find they were pleased by my interest in their history. Like Dante with Virgil, I was grateful I had found a guide and companion in Louisa Anne Meredith.

In going to Tasmania, not only was I about to do something my father never imagined I would or could, I also had my own kind of love affair to pursue. There were other links too. Connections with *The Tempest* were working away in my subconscious. John Lucas in his introduction to *Cutting the Clouds Towards* (the collection's title is a phrase from the play suggesting flying in the direction of) commented that I was 'throughout aware of, may be said to be haunted by, another island discovered, another father lost and transformed, other voices set free.' On top of this, I couldn't help remembering that the anonymous 'Ballad of Van Diemen's Land' (Van Diemen's Land being the earlier name for Tasmania) had an alternative title, 'You Rambling Boys of Liverpool', and one of its verses runs:

> As I lay in the hold one night
>   A-dreaming all alone
> I dreamed I was in Liverpool,
>   Way back in my old home
> With my true love beside me
>   And a jug of ale in hand,
> When I woke quite broken-hearted
>   Lying off Van Diemen's Land.

And there was dirty Maggie May too, and all those other unfortunates from the 'criminal classes' shipped to the other side of the world. There were the crimes of imperialism to confront. As well as the barbaric treatment of the shipped-out convicts, there was the attempted eradication of the Aboriginal people, for which I found echoes in Prospero's treatment of Caliban ('This island's mine which thou tak'st from me'). Much as there was to admire in Louisa Anne, she was also a product of her times and she displays attitudes (however liberal-minded she thought herself to be) one is obliged to put in the debit column. She and I had our disagreements, a spirited exchange of views. At one point I have her accuse me of 'the arrogance of hindsight'. In a poem called 'Making an Exhibition' she rounds on me:

> So that's what you think!
>
> No chance for me to plead
> rawness of the time,
> uncompromising place –
> the *scenery* that you applaud
> from cars,
>
> nor slovenly rum-glazed servants,
> larders treacle-black with flies,
> molestations of the elements,
> feral bushrangers, fierceness
> of the dispossessed?
>
> > Be sure
> your rightness isn't just for display.
> No time-and-place is ever
> without guilts and shames.
> We are all victims of something…

One reviewer saw it in these terms: 'In neither shirking this re-creation of the imperialist vision nor accepting it uncritically, Simpson has created a context in which contemporary sensibilities have a sounding board, giving a resonance beyond even that which the not inconsiderable craft of his writing could provide on its own.'[4] Be that last clause as it may, this was certainly something I was hoping I might achieve in the poems. Anyone with an interest in this 'imperialist vision' as it affected life in Tasmania should read Robert Hughes's passionate and masterly *Fatal*

Shore (another quotation from 'The Ballad of Van Diemen's Land') and Matthew Kneale's excellent novel *English Passengers*.[5]

The residency lasted for two months, with a week either side spent in Melbourne, during the first of which I ran a workshop (one of the students in it had been born in my home town of Bootle) and gave a reading at La Trobe University; the second (my final week) was spent staying with the fine Greek/Australian poet, Dimitris Tsaloumas.[6]

It was in that first week in Melbourne that I was shown a copy of Vivienne Rae Ellis's biography of Louisa Anne Meredith.[7] Seeing photographs of her for the first time started the poetic conversations up again. I wrote a poem called 'We Meet at Last'.

> We meet at Warrandyte,
> the good professor's house
>
> where distant bell birds ping
> and magpies chortle in
>
> the pepper trees.
> I mean I get to see
>
> a frontispiece. The *carte*
> *de visite* photographer
>
> has gone for that soft-focus
> pre-Raphaelite look
>
> the men all like:
> that studied ambivalence,
>
> *noli me tangere* yet
> *console me in my hour of need...*

Other photographs, including one of her husband, Charles, are reprinted in *Cutting the Clouds Towards.*

Another 22 poems were written during the residency and these were collected in a booklet, *On the Right Side of the Earth*, published by the Queen Victoria Museum and Art Gallery. Most of them were written in the Artist's Cottage in Launceston. The setting could not have been more idyllic or imposing, situated at the entrance to Cataract Gorge through whose brown crags the South Esk River flows. Possums clattered in the rafters all night and during the day skinks scurried across the floorboards. The cottage is possibly the most photographed building on Tasmania and several times a day a strange little tourist paddleboat chugs past it. I would sometimes stand on my balcony and wave regally at its passengers.

One must be careful with coincidences, and not treat them superstitiously. I have already suggested that this experience I was undergoing was somehow *meant*. The trouble is one can't help – especially when they keep coming at you thick and fast – relishing coincidences, not least from a poetic point of view; finding and making links and patterns is a way of securing meaning and promoting significance.

I met, for example, several metamorphoses of Prospero during my stay on the island. The only play performed at the small Princess Theatre in Launceston while I was there was *The Tempest*. Then one of the students in a workshop I conducted at the University of Tasmania was called Arielle. In the tiny Maritime Museum in Hobart I saw a photograph of a ship, the *Glen McDonald*, my father had sailed in a long time ago; on the evening of the same day, at a reading I gave in the Bavarian Tavern in (wait for it) Liverpool Street, I met a lookalike who, for a split second, seemed to confirm my father's having set more than just a foot there – that is until the lookalike said in a thick German accent that his name was Otto! (My wife is German and during the residency her mother died in Berlin.)

On my first evening in Launceston, I was taken to a restaurant where I met a young poet, Anthony Lawrence, over from the mainland to take part in the Tasmanian Poetry Festival that coincided with the first week of the residency. We were introduced and Anthony Lawrence's first words were 'Matt Simpson? *You* got me started!' I had come 12,000 miles to discover a poet – and a good one at that – claiming me as a formative influence! For the final presentation of the residency, the Queen Victoria Museum and Art Gallery (two weeks after the centenary of Louisa Anne's death in Melbourne) sent out invitations, and two replies came from a 'Mrs Meredith'. I thought I was being leg-pulled and could name at least two people who were almost certainly having me on. But in the event, one of the Mrs Merediths was genuine – a tall, stern-looking elderly lady who had not been pleased when I said at the start of my reading 'Would the real Mrs Meredith please stand up'!

While I was away I read as many of Mrs Meredith's publications as I could lay my hands on and never lost my admiration for her undaunted courage in the dangerous and disheartening times of her life, for the enviable exactness of her observations of the natural world around her (she was also a very gifted water-colourist) and for her genteel but spiky humour. I visited the several different houses she lived in along the east coast of the island and met people who had memorabilia and stories to tell.

Tasmania then was a place psychologically and poetically reached for – it was part of my odyssey. At least when I stood on the quayside at Hobart I could say *Look, dad, I got here too, there's no further argument, no need for accusations, you came here in your right, I in mine, we're all square.*

In 1999 I guest-read on an Arvon course at Lumb Bank, and in conversing with one of the students afterwards I was delighted to find that she had understood the psychological dynamics of the poetry. She spoke about it in Jungian terms, using the word 'synchronicity' to describe the coincidences that occurred along the way and clearly saw that, though I was going to Tasmania to talk, as it were, to the ghost of my father, I was also pursuing a female figure, Louisa Anne. I will admit that Jung was among my early influences and it is no problem for me to push the Jungian further and talk of the integration of the animus and anima aspects of the personality.

In the title poem to my first collection, 'Making Arrangements', I had written:

> I think perhaps
> it's time to gauge whatever love
> there was or might have been, or time
> to ask the dead to let me estimate
> their suffering by the yardstick of my flesh,
> time at last to come home to myself.

When I wrote that, reflecting on the deaths of both my parents, I imagined that I was making a statement. As it turned out, it was a prediction. It was in Tasmania that I felt I had at least glimpsed the possibility of what it meant to come home to oneself. It was, in the words of one of the poems in *Cutting the Clouds Towards*, 'almost what I'd come for' – a line from a poem, which, in the words of John Lucas's introduction, has a 'necessarily ambiguous title'. That title is 'About as Far as We Can Go'. Here are the closing lines:

> It was a moment, almost what
> I'd come for, which was to meet
> and greet the you-in-me, bosun,
> in Salamanca Place.

Whatever the case, the enterprise did receive a blessing of a sort. In a part of Tasmania aptly called Flowerdale, Barney Roberts, the grand old man of Tasmanian letters, farms with two of his sons. His daughter-in-law, Jo, had a cruel sense of humour – very similar to Liverpool humour – challenging, ferreting out and excoriating the slightest hint of pretension. She was determined to search me out. Barney was 75 when I visited him and was – and still is – as tough, in a sort of Robert Frost way, as they come. He writes poetry but his main claim to fame is two fine books of short stories and a celebrated account of his wartime experiences. He was for sure one of my father-figure Prosperos and I ended up writing a poem for him to express my gratitude for the generosity of his hospitality, company and conversation. Jo demanded to read it, looking for and expecting to find Pommie bullshit, but once she'd read it she came over and quietly kissed me on the cheek. It was at that moment I felt I had really 'arrived'.

The poems in *Cutting the Clouds Towards* are divided into two sections – those written in England before the residency and those written during it. (A couple were in fact written later, back in Liverpool.) The second section is introduced with the epigraph from *The Tempest:* 'For he is sure i' th' island'. There is a prologue about a ship in a bottle that my father made while away at sea, and there is an epilogue, which details my vain attempt to find Louisa Anne's grave in Melbourne Central Cemetery. This epilogue ends:

Last chance and something of
an off-chance, even if it bites the dust,
leaves ashes in the mouth, I mean
for me to pay respects.

Sunday, cemetery office shut,
no hope of documentary help,
map to show me your last bit
of colonising. Blow flies, blow flies

everywhere, nostrils, mouth. And so
I scuff cindery paths
round battered stones, hop
over rusted rails in Death's

neglected territory, the older
graves that say *This is the mark*

we came to make. But you
I cannot stumble on in time.

You're here somewhere, not
talking, not anything. I head out past
new immigrant Italian polished marble.
Who says Magnificence is dead?

Men, women down on knees,
washing, buffing dry, meticulous
with flowers, coddling their dead
as if just love might keep them near.

*

I tried my best. But time's a bully.
There are clouds to cut, Louisa Anne.

Notes

1   *Cutting the Clouds Towards* is Matt Simpson's fourth full-length collection of
    poems. It was published by Liverpool University Press in 1998.
2   Dale Spender (ed.), *The Penguin Anthology of Australian Women's Writing*,
    Harmondsworth, Penguin, 1988.
3   Louisa Anne Meredith, *Notes and Sketches of New South Wales* (1844), repr.
    Harmondsworth, Penguin, 1973.
4   Tim Thorne, *Island – 79*, winter 1999.
5   Robert Hughes, *The Fatal Shore*, London, Pan Books, 1988; Matthew Kneale,
    English Passengers, Harmondsworth, Penguin, 2001.
6   Matt Simpson and John Lucas have co-edited a selection of the poetry of
    Dimitris Tsaloumas entitled *Stoneland Harvest*, Nottingham, Shoestring
    Press, 1999.
7   Vivienne Rae Ellis, *Louisa Anne Meredith – A Tigress in Exile*, Hobart, Tasmania,
    St David's Park Publishing, 1979.

INTERVIEWS

Adrian Henri

Singer of Meat and Flowers

David Bateman

Adrian Henri's major achievements are as a poet and a painter, and his sheer versatility in the arts helped to transform the popular impression of British poetry in the 1960s. His cultural eclecticism and his organising ability and enthusiasm were key elements in making the 1960s Liverpool poetry explosion happen the way it did.

The huge range of his influences and his deliberate changes of style have resulted in some unevenness in his own work, and he has frequently been damned with faint praise. Yet the best of his poetry, from the 1960s through to his most recent publications, presents highly individual fusions of public and private worlds.

Adrian Henri's poetry, more so than that of Roger McGough or Brian Patten, is particularly redolent of Liverpool: local references and place-names abound, and his poetry creates a Liverpool that is both ordinary and magical, everyday and legendary. Heavily inspired by New York Beat poet Allen Ginsberg, Adrian Henri brings home William Blake's vision of Albion: an England of heroic optimism as well as tedium and hypocrisy, and where the mythical exists within the commonplace, just waiting to be seen.

However, Henri in his early poems is also emphatically a pop poet. The opening (and closing) lines of 'Mrs Albion You've Got A Lovely Daughter' are full of youth, excitement, sexuality and Liverpool:

> Albion's most lovely daughter sat on the banks of the Mersey
> dangling her landing stage into the water.

The daughters of Albion
> arriving by underground at Central Station
> eating hot ecclescakes at the Pierhead
> writing 'Billy Blake is fab' on a wall in Mathew St

taking off their navyblue schooldrawers and
putting on nylon panties ready for the night...

Beautiful boys with bright red guitars
in the spaces between the stars

Reelin' an' a-rockin'
Wishin' an' a-hopin'
Kissin' an' a-prayin'
Lovin' an' a-layin'

Mrs Albion you've got a lovely daughter.

Adrian Henri's poems are mostly love poems, autobiographical snippets
and collages full of bright and dark sensual detail; others are wry little
observations and wordplays, often a bit funny, often poignant. Others,
with various intentions, experiment with forms, including a last will and
testament, advertisements, short stories and stage directions; and some
are flights of fantasy, bringing great buffetings of apocalyptic imagery or
setting characters from fiction and myth in the everyday world.

    Some of Henri's poems are of little but autobiographical interest;
sometimes he relies too heavily on a mere listing of objects to convey
emotion, which can give a long-winded, prosaic feel; and some of his
more experimental poems simply misfire. These are three of the reasons
why Henri has attracted even more critical flak than his two Mersey
Sound compadres. Four further reasons can equally be seen as
strengths: first, his very explicit cultural eclecticism; second, his
repeated themes and obsessions (including, for example, the persistent
references to panties, images which his harsher critics seem particularly
unable to remove from their minds); third, his ability (along
with McGough) to inject humour into serious themes; and last but
possibly not least, the fact that he stayed in the city he has written
most about.

Spitfires and Fairgrounds, Skulls and Flowers

Adrian Henri was born in Tranmere, Birkenhead in 1932, and moved to
Rhyl on the North Wales coast in 1938. His drawing ability emerged as
early as primary school: 'I was a fat, bespectacled child, and I used to get
bullied. But it was during the war, and I could draw realistic Spitfires
and Hurricanes and Messerschmitts and things, so that was my way of

avoiding being bullied, really, by drawing for kids in the playground.'
Later he joined the Rhyl Children's Theatre Club, taking minor acting
and singing roles, and being in charge of scenery design. From sec-
ondary modern school, where he was 'this hopeless figure… completely
a square peg in a round hole',[1] the 13+ test enabled Henri to move to
the grammar school in the tiny 'city' of St Asaph five miles to the south.
Here he first met Philip Jones Griffiths, who would become a photogra-
pher and a long-term friend, and here he also eventually excelled at art,
English and French, developing enthusiasms for Picasso, Magritte,
Matisse, Pound, Eliot, Rimbaud and Baudelaire. He began working
summers on the stalls and rides of Rhyl's fairground: 'it was where I
really started to learn about language, slang and dialect, and another
tremendous confidence builder.'[2]

In 1951 Henri went to King's College, Newcastle (University of
Durham) to study fine art. His lecturers included Lawrence Gowing,
Roger de Grey, Victor Pasmore and Richard Hamilton; and the 'Euston
Road School' realist influence of Gowing and de Grey (themselves influ-
enced by early Pasmore) is evident in Henri's college efforts. Hamilton's
collage-work and proto-pop art would become a very direct and power-
ful influence on Henri following his visit to the 'This Is Tomorrow' exhi-
bition in late summer 1956, as Henri himself emphasises (see p. 85).
Pasmore's influence was more in his openness to new approaches: long
established as a painter of naturalistic landscapes and interiors, in 1948
he began turning to non-figurative geometrical paintings; in 1949 he
added collage to his techniques; and in 1950–51 he produced the first of
many geometrical projective reliefs. Witnessing the results of these
developments at close quarters, Adrian Henri was profoundly impressed
by Pasmore's apparently overnight transformation in theoretical
approach and his new-found versatility in techniques. Until 1955,
though, Henri's painting was fairly staid, and his own versatility in the
arts stretched mostly just to playing washboard, and occasionally
singing, with the King's College Jazz Band.

Graduating in 1955, Henri took a one-year art-teaching job in
Preston, where he met Joyce Wilson at Preston Jazz Club. His summer
work at Rhyl resulted in meetings with Mike Evans, later a poet and
member of the Liverpool Scene, and also Alan Blease, who tempted
Henri to move to Liverpool, where he worked initially as a scenic artist
for the Playhouse. Joyce and Adrian married in 1957 and Adrian taught
in schools until 1960, followed by part-time lecturing in Manchester
(1961–64) then Liverpool College of Art (1964–68). 1958 and 1959 saw

the first three exhibitions of his work, including the Five Painters exhibition at the Bluecoat which also featured Anthony Collinge, Henry Graham, Don McKinlay and Alan Wood.

Adrian Henri began visiting Streate's Coffee Bar on May Street, Mount Pleasant, where Johnny Byrne ran regular poetry and jazz nights. Here he met poets Pete Brown and Spike Hawkins, and it was Brown who introduced Henri to Roger McGough in December 1960. Just under a year later at Streate's, Brian Patten read his poetry for the first time, and in the following week met first McGough at Streate's, then Henri. Though Henri was frequenting poetry events, he didn't see himself as a poet at this time, keeping to himself the poetry that he wrote 'every so often... with no real purpose in mind', as had done since the sub-Eliot 'adolescent poems of rejection' of his college days. On the other hand he was finding his own visual language in his urban images, in which his frequent pop-art appropriation of commercial images contained an ordinariness, a downmarket quality lacking in the work of his American counterparts. Many of these visual pieces would themselves directly provide material for his poetry: *Death Of A Bird In The City* (1961); *Fairground Images* (1961, 1962); *Père Ubu In Liverpool* (1962); *The Entry Of Christ Into Liverpool* (1962–64); and the *Liverpool 8* sequence (1963–64). The monstrous character of Père Ubu, a sort of cross between Macbeth and Mr Punch (and originally the anti-hero of three plays by Alfred Jarry), would turn up particularly frequently in Henri's poetry and pictures. Transposed to Liverpool, this international psychopath would become a more hapless character, and would also become a virtual alter ego for Henri much as he had been for Jarry at the end of the nineteenth century.

In the first half of 1962 Henri read an article by New York artist Allan Kaprow on 'happenings', and having already made assemblages, he was keen to organise Britain's first such events. The first, 'City', took place around August, and various others followed. Henri writes:

> The happenings were presented as part of a Merseyside Arts Festival in 1962 and 1963, along with poetry-and-music and folk-evenings. The 'events', as we called them, quickly became a popular form of entertainment: a mixture of poetry, rock'n'roll, and assemblage. The early ones like 'City' (1962), by Henri/John Gorman/Roger McGough, used a taped music track. Later events had live music by local 'Merseybeat' groups, for instance the Roadrunners and the Clayton Squares, as in 'Nightblues', 1963.[3]

As a visual artist, Adrian Henri was now making direct use of his imme-
diate surroundings; and as an events organiser, artist and sometimes
compère, he was fusing various arts and making use of his showmanly
skills first learned in plays and fairgrounds. His awareness of wider cul-
ture, coupled with his enthusiasm and quickly learned organising abil-
ity, made him a prime mover in the development of the early 1960s
Liverpool poetry scene, taking it speedily from its low-key jazz-cafe
homes to a range of new environments, not only creating the vitally
important association of poetry with pop music, but also setting up
events that fused poetry and music with visual art, drama, comedy and
audience participation.

What is perhaps surprising is that he had kept his own poetry private
and separate from all this, until his somewhat belated first public read-
ing at Sampson & Barlow's. His own account of this performance shows
a naive lack of street-wisdom at that time (see p. 82), but also a quick-
ness to learn from experience in finding his own poetic voice.

Once he'd started, he didn't waste time. A great deal of his subject
matter was ready-made insofar as his poetic concerns were the same as
his artistic ones: urban life, ordinary life and its disruption by extra-
ordinary mythological intrusions. These might be the entry of Christ
into Liverpool (after James Ensor's painting *The Entry of Christ into Brus-
sels*); a vision of a city bursting into flower; or simply ordinary, extraor-
dinary everyday love. The latter included his 1964 meeting with student
Heather Holden and the beginning of a relationship which had to be
kept secret from his employers though not from Joyce, with whom
Heather established a lasting friendship.

Yet what is often overlooked is Adrian Henri's application of visual art
theory to the writing of poetry. Besides the sheer visual quality of his
poetry and the pop-art use of commercial everyday objects, there is his
Warholian wholesale appropriation of styles and even texts presented as
new poems; the constant use of collage techniques; and in relation to
Kaprow, the constant overlapping of poetry with other arts.

Out of the people involved in the events and poetry readings in 1963,
a theatrical satire group also formed, presenting combinations of
sketches, music and poetry at pubs and theatres. This was the *Liverpool
One Fat Lady All Electric Show*, centred around McGough, Gorman, Henri,
Mike McGear (McCartney) and Jenny Beattie. From these five, an ABC
TV audition in 1964 selected McGough, Gorman and McGear, thus
defining the incipient Scaffold. This resulted in Adrian Henri working
on his later events more closely with Brian Patten, and developing a

closer working relationship with Mike Evans of the Clayton Squares and Mike Hart of the Roadrunners. Adrian Henri finally linked his modicum of blues-singing experience with his poetry, and gradually a poetry-and-music group was formed, centred around Henri, Evans, Hart and Andy Roberts. Following the publication, in March 1967, of Edward Lucie-Smith's anthology of Liverpool poetry,[4] the group became known simply as the Liverpool Scene.

The Liverpool Scene played pop, folk, jazz and blues, toured extensively and released five LPs of their poetry and music. Working with the group took up most of Henri's time for three years. Inevitably this diverted his energies from his other writing and his painting, but it also gave him a chance to explore some of those lyric idioms he had already used in his poetry. Two spoof numbers particularly stand out: 'The Woo Woo', supposedly a cover song dedicated to its originators, the early rhythm-and-blues group Bobby & The Helmets, 'who are tragically with us no more'; and a mickey-take of the southern England blues boom, 'I've Got Those Fleetwood Mac Chicken Shack John Mayall Can't Fail Blues'.

Following a financially unsuccessful USA tour in late 1969, there were increasing tensions within the Liverpool Scene. Some of the arguments were about Henri's disproportionately large share of the publicity; others were about musical direction as Evans and Percy Jones wanted to move more towards jazz while Henri and Roberts wanted to continue their eclectic approach. The arguments got uglier, and in April 1970 the Liverpool Scene broke up. In May, Adrian Henri's maternal grandparents died, and in June his own parents died. He himself had a heart attack in August, necessitating a long convalescence. 'It literally changed all my thinking, and what I was, I suppose, really... I was literally a different person into 1971 from what I had been in 1969.' A more sombre and introspective Adrian Henri appears in *Autobiography* (1971) and several of his later works. The 1970 poem 'Morning Song' has its lust for life (and plain lust) tempered and sharpened by its night-time awareness of 'the body's process /.../ The unfamiliar pounding that may cease at any moment.'

For various reasons, then, Henri himself moved on from the areas he had opened up; and for various reasons (including the divergence of pop into chart records and progressive rock), there were few others to take up the pop-poetry baton at that time, so the fusion of poetry and pop was arguably never truly consolidated until the appearance of the new wave and dub poets of the late 1970s. However, those dub poets themselves have been quick to acknowledge their debt to the Liverpool poetry of the 1960s.

This is not to say that Adrian Henri abandoned combined arts formats. The Grimms tours of the early 1970s were followed by a Liverpool Scene revival tour in 1974, and he frequently worked with musicians thereafter (including the rhythm-and-blues band Lawnmower and the Royal Liverpool Philharmonic Orchestra). His interest in performance art continued, including the somewhat premature 'Funeral Of Adrian Henri' (1979). New directions included novel writing, play writing, and – notably in the 1980s and 1990s – writing for children.

Visual art always had an enormous influence on Henri's poetry, and it is worth considering his poetry in the same way we would consider conceptual visual art. Manufactured images portray 'real life', and become part of it, but also affect our reactions to the things they portray, as in the exclaimed single line of 'Lakeland Poem 1': 'The landscape is full of other people's paintings!' On the one hand this is simply a variation on the old quip about *Macbeth* being full of quotes; but on the other, it shows art turning nature as well as itself into cliché. Any clear boundary between pop-art and nature poetry is lost in a world where the seasonality of plastic daffodils has already suggested that daffodils themselves are not real. Thus the thought of laying plastic daffodils at Wordsworth's grave is not a simple satire; and what begins as a simple paradox has lasting reverberations through Henri's work, subtly affecting his later flower symbolisms. A fusing of opposites is found again in Henri's use of meat and bone: the meat in 'Meat Poem' and 'Morning Song' is very much living meat (as it is in Patten's poem 'Meat'); and living skeletons are a repeated image in Henri's paintings and poetry, sometimes as threatening figures and sometimes simply as companions of the living.

There is a surprising unity and continuity in Adrian Henri's use of such an immense range of influences. There are the daffodils from Wordsworth and from Woolworths (and from city councils and from packets of Omo) throughout his 1960s work; but the skeletons are a more persistent example. They first appeared as the risen dead in *The Entry Of Christ Into Liverpool,* and were inspired by Henri's reading about the Basle Festival in Switzerland as much as by James Ensor or the Bible; after 1970 they reappear, but more threateningly, as classic guises of death in 'The Dance Of Death' and 'The Triumph Of Death'; then the Eliot-inspired poem 'Wasteland' has its 'Rats' Alley/ where the dead men snatch handbags'; the 'skeleton hand' of Death 'painted in the manner of Hans Holbein' appears briefly but mortally in 'A Portrait Of The Artist'; and most recently, skeletons appear as unthreatening figures again in *The Day Of The Dead, Hope Street*, inspired by José Guadalupe Posada's woodcuts of the Mexican celebration. Here, the skeletons, some singing and dancing, accompany the living representations of Henri's memories of his dead heroes, friends and wife.

The presence of Liverpool in much of Adrian Henri's poetry is part of the strong sense of place throughout his work. Adrian Henri has a passion for the particular, be it street names, brands of washing powder or species of plant (and here is part of the continuity between pop-artist and nature artist). The early poems include not only Liverpool but also a touring poet's impressions of Edinburgh and later the USA. Some of these early travel-influenced pieces are concerned with local impressions and little else, but Adrian Henri's more recent globetrotting provided contexts for more purposeful poetic intentions, as in 'I Have Woken This Year', 'Wish You Were Here' and the *Yosemite* sequence for Catherine Marcangeli.

With the notable (and notably American) exception of 'Batman', politics is mostly only ever implicit in Adrian Henri's 1960s and 1970s poetry. *Autobiography* (1971) was written when Henri was full of anger and guilt at the neglectful way his grandparents had been treated after their lifetime of work, and was intended to be explicitly political; but except when writing of urban neglect in 'Poem For Liverpool 8', or of wanting 'to make everyone know/ to change the world' in 'Poem For Hugh MacDiarmid', any political messages are kept implicit. The poem 'Shadowland' takes a very different approach. *Wish You Were Here* (1990) is a poignant collection, the death in 1987 of Joyce Henri its recurring theme; and 'Shadowland', the second-to-last poem in the book, is a sudden hammer-blow. Imperfectly crafted and sometimes reliant on cliché, this is nevertheless a powerful, near-surreal, multi-voiced encapsulation of the Thatcherite state: 'a whole nation for sale/ with only history to offer...' The theme of heritage as betrayal is returned to in 'End Of The Road', one of several political poems in the 'Look, Stranger...' section of *Not Fade Away* (1994); one of the effects of this grouping is to subtly draw attention to the latent political aspects of the poems alongside them. 'The Grandmothers', within its gently sad fairy-tale setting, is a frighteningly literal parable of neglect, and a fierce release of the anger and guilt pent up in the earlier *Autobiography.* Yet for all the darkness of the political poems in *Not Fade Away*, there is optimism and humour too; Henri's habitual dusky autumnal leanings are balanced by a freshness and optimism reflecting its dedication to his new love, Catherine Marcangeli.

In June 1998, Adrian Henri suffered a major heart attack. This only briefly put a halt to his writing, painting and performing; but a heart bypass operation in January 1999 was followed by two strokes in February and hospitalisation for six months, initially with the prognosis that he would probably never walk or talk again. In February 2000 he had just begun writing poetry again: 'I'm a very different me from the one about a year ago... I'm starting to do, sort of, "post-stroke poems," I suppose you might say.' Adrian Henri died on 10 April 2000, only a short time after this interview.

Background to the Interview

The interview, which is here chopped around so as to present it in roughly biographical order, took place at Adrian Henri's house in Mount Street, Liverpool, on 12 February 2000. Round the corner on Hardman Street, there were banners with pink hearts advertising the Adrian Henri exhibition which had opened just the previous week at the Walker Art Gallery. Catherine Marcangeli was getting ready to go the Philharmonic Hall to work on arrangements for the Adrian Henri tribute evening on 21 March, at which the Scaffold, Brian Patten, Carol Ann Duffy, George Melly, Andy Roberts, Willy Russell, Alan Bleasdale and others would be appearing. Also at the Philharmonic, his oratorio *Lowlands Away* was due for performance on 1 March. I asked him if it had been hectic with the opening and everything. 'Oh yeah,' he says. 'Yeah. It's been marvellous.'

Earliest Poems, Performance and Publication

DB: Had you been writing some poetry for a while before moving into Liverpool?

AH: Intermittently, yes. And it was strictly the kind of thing, you shut your eyes and then keep in a drawer, and don't show to anybody, you know. And when I began, it was like, very very pastiche T. S. Eliot, because I fell under the spell of Eliot completely when I was in the sixth form. And I wrote long, turgid, mock-Eliot sort of things: a cross between T. S. Eliot and teenage angst, really. And I went on doing that for about ten years, I suppose, and just keeping them and not doing anything.

DB: Where was the first place where you did poetry live? Was that at Streate's?

AH: I never really did Streate's. That was Johnny Byrne and
Pete Brown, and people like that. I mean I started seriously doing
it in Sampson & Barlow's, in London Road. We had a once-a-
week thing.

   And it was when I started – I was more of an organiser than a poet,
really, for the Sampson & Barlow's readings; I was helping out,
and Roger and Brian said, You write things, and I said, Well not
really, and they said, Well, why don't you try them out? And it was
one of the most defining moments in my life, really, because I
stood up and read this thing that I thought was so wonderful, and it
was in fact acutely embarrassing, because it was an audience of
sceptical Scousers with a pint in their hand, you know, and I'm
muttering all this thing with quotations and whatever. And I just
realised that this wasn't working at all. So I went away; and I
actually – I didn't rewrite things, but I just thought, well okay, that's
behind me; and I've got to do something simple and direct and able
to be understood at one sitting. So it was a quite conscious decision
on my part to do it that way, really. It was just so embarrassing,
I remember.

   So, if I look back at it, all the early poems that were in anthologies,
and the Liverpool poets book and whatever, that's all mostly from
then to mid-1966, really, I suppose. Once I'd started, I couldn't stop.
But it was just finding a voice.

DB: What were the key things in finding your voice at that time?

AH: Well, we were very conscious that people like Michael Horovitz
and Pete Brown – well, not those two, but there were lesser people,
who always had a mid-Atlantic accent because they were hung up
on Beat poetry and things; and so they imagined that if they
sounded like Allen Ginsberg or Jack Kerouac or whatever, then that
was somehow okay. That was the thing. And I remember, several
times actually, discussing this and saying, well, that's all very
well, you know: if you come from Paterson, New Jersey or Kansas
City or wherever, then you work in your particular voice. And what
it seemed to me, and Roger and Brian, I think, was that, somehow
or other, our voice was the voice of Liverpool, or the voice you're
given, really. So it was more honest to actually just do it in your
own voice. And then the corollary of that, I suppose, was that you
started to find your own voice, and ultimately use it almost as a
medium to say things. So in our different ways I think we all came
to the same conclusion, which is that we didn't want to do it like

Brown, Horovitz and all those – I thought it was effete Southerners – who were doing that mid-Atlantic thing. And what we all in our different ways came to realise is that you use your own voice. And if you look at Ginsberg and you look at William Carlos Williams or whatever, that's exactly what they were doing, except they were doing it in terms of Paterson, New Jersey, or whatever, not in terms of Liverpool.

So it was a question of, how do I do this in my own way, that is in the Modernist tradition? But... I suppose I'm always haunted by Modernism, in a way that neither McGough nor Patten are really, in the sense of Père Ubu and things like that; there are hints of Alfred Jarry and all sorts of other things in what I wrote at the time.

But some of it, I felt that if it worked in a sort of project, in a context, that people would believe in, then it was all right. Say, this poem about Ubu walking past the Kardomah... At a tangent to that, the other thing I noticed, right at the front of this thing [indicating new catalogue], they've got a copy of an old poem called 'I Want to Paint', and I realised that what the important thing about it was, I suppose, other than the jokes, that it was actually all the things you couldn't paint.

DB: It's a poem of wild dreams, isn't it?

AH: Yeah. Yeah, you know, and it's... 'A SYSTEMATIC DERANGE-MENT OF ALL THE SENSES' printed miles high over Liverpool, and things. So it was all these impossible things, things that you couldn't possibly paint. That seemed to be a fun idea to put them all together somehow.

DB: What sparked off that poem?

AH: I think it was just that. I think it was just the idea of impossible paintings. It started from that really. And I also had Part 1 and Part 2, cos I thought it would be like one of those James Brown records, where you've got so-and-so Part 1, and then you turn the record over, and it's so-and-so Part 2.

DB: Like a single, yeah.

AH: Yeah. So it's also a distant reminiscence of that as well, I suppose.

DB: When was your poetry first published anywhere?

AH: I think, of all places, it was the TLS, actually.

DB: [astonished] Sorry? The TLS, did you say?

AH: Yeah. [brief pause for the laughter to subside] It was 'Talking After Christmas Blues'. And at the time, John Willett was assistant editor of the TLS, and he took it in to them. I don't know how he did, really, because Ian Hamilton was the poetry editor, and he was absolutely vehemently opposed to anything to do with Liverpool and Liverpool poets; but somehow or other, Willett managed to smuggle this in. So there was that one, and then a poem called 'In Memoriam, T. S. Eliot': that got published in the TLS as well. And while all this was going on, Patten had run this amazingly successful little magazine called *Underdog*. And all the best poems I had eventually appeared in *Underdog*.

DB: Anyway, I was interested to find out when you were first published, and I'm just staggered to find out that it was in the TLS…

AH: Yeah. I don't know. When I think about it now, it is, I suppose, a bit of an achievement, really.

DB: Also, it's deeply ironic, considering its reaction to *The Liverpool Scene* and *The Mersey Sound*.

AH: Yeah, exactly.

DB: That must have been very hurtful…

AH: Oh yeah. I mean, you laugh about it, but… You know, actors say, like, 'I don't read my notices,' but I'm sure they do. And I know that it hurt. Because you were doing something that you felt was important, and you were just being rubbished. And when Hamilton – at one point he used to review anonymously in the TLS, and under his own name in the *New Statesman* or something, and also occasionally when he got in a little magazine… So you could actually get what seemed like three different dismissive notices, from apparently different people; and in fact it was the same person.

DB: A bit nasty.

AH: Yeah. So it was not a happy situation, really.

Visual Art, English Poetry and Happenings

DB: To do with visual art, and its relation to your poetry, I remember once asking you if you were trying to do, with some of your poetry, what Warhol had done by appropriating images; and you were saying, Yeah. And you were saying there were various painters who'd influenced the way that you approached poetry. Who were those, and how did they influence you?

AH: I think the post-abstract generation of painting in America, like Jim Dine and Rauschenberg and Jasper Johns, and particularly the man who invented 'happenings', Allan Kaprow. I think I got a whole lot of stuff from him, and from them, generically. I was almost doing a Liverpool version of what I thought Rauschenberg was doing in

New York. And then I learned about Kaprow doing happenings and things, which I wanted to try out, and did.

DB: Which particular poems most purely illustrate the Rauschenberg influence?

AH: Almost any one of those collage poems; the ones where they depend on paradox... I mean, there are references to Rauschenberg anyway, in at least two poems, I think. But I met Jim Dine, briefly, because he'd done a Happening called 'Car Crash'. When I did a thing called 'Car Crash Blues', it was dedicated to Jim Dine.

So I think that although there are other influences like, obviously James Ensor, and Jarry, I suppose, with the graphic works, probably the main influence really – oh, and I suppose the other thing is that I was taught briefly by Richard Hamilton, and it was when I was a final year student, and he was getting us to do collages and things, which I thought were fun, but it wasn't Art. You know, Art was what you do with oil paint and turps and all things like that. And it was only after I'd left college, and I saw a wonderful exhibition in London called 'This Is Tomorrow'; there were various artists and architects doing it; and the classic one was Richard Hamilton where he had Robby the Robot from *Forbidden Planet*, and all that, and at that point it sort of clicked to me, that what he was about wasn't just, like, fun-having with bits of paper, you know, messing about with bits of paper, but was actually Art, and doing it another way.

It's amazing, cos I was aware of people like Schwitters, and people like that, but I wasn't aware of the fact that that could apply to me: I was a painter, and that was all there was to it. And the fact was, that it was something that could extend and grow...

So there were important influences apart from the American ones, but I think the main ones were from America, really.

DB: It strikes me that visual art is very important to your poetry in at least two different ways: one is the emphasis on physical description, the visual quality to them; but also there's a lot of structural ways in which they're influenced. Like, you mentioned collage as being one particular thing, and I think you use that a lot, for example in 'The Entry Of Christ...' – in fact, that uses lots of different images put together at once, and it's left for the reader to put it together.

AH: Yeah. I think at one point on which I actually decided that whatever happened, I didn't want to write English poetry; so it was a question of, How do I do it if I don't do that? So eventually I did

'Last Will and Testament', and, I suppose, 'I Want to Paint'… There were some, I think, that have now perished, that were, sort of, like, you give out to an audience and you know, say take it away and ask them to do it within the next five days or something. So I think I was always trying to point… that British poetry as it was, which was then The Group, and so on, was so narrow-minded, and devious, and sort of xenophobic, I suppose. Like, you don't respect anything that's not written in your language. And even then, a lot of those guys were working in very classical English-poetry sorts of ways: I mean sonnets and whatever. And I just decided that I didn't want to do that, whatever happened; I was clear there was another way of doing it: whether by inventing my own form, like 'Last Will and Testament'; or by using collage, or pop song, or blues-based material, using forms that were common to everybody, not just specialists in literature.

DB: What were the key similarities and key differences between your own events and the happenings that sparked them off?

AH: I think what we hit on, unconsciously, was that music was a very important issue, somehow. Because – well, all of the first ones, we did to a soundtrack. So we were actually specifying, you know, a bit of that, a bit of that, and whatever; we would do it all on tape. And the time of the event was when the music finished, as it were.

The first few were just recorded sounds, and then I got together with a band called the Roadrunners, and we did a couple of things like that. And then there was a band called the Clayton Squares. And I think we did… The last of the real happenings were done at the Cavern Club. So we did one called 'Bomb', which was a sort of anti-nuclear protest poem event, and then we did a thing called 'The Black and White Show', which was anti-apartheid. So the last things we did, as such, were the most politicised, in a way.

DB: Did the last ones all include a combination of visual art, music, poetry, drama…?

AH: Yeah. It was very much a mélange of all those things.

DB: Would you say that that mix was usually successful?

AH: Yeah. It was, actually. I mean, I think it was a sort of phase… I mean it's very interesting that all the people like Jim Dine, Claes Oldenburg and people like that had all had a go at doing that, and had moved on. I wouldn't say that was, like, good, but I don't know. Something, in a way, told me that we'd gone as far as we could go with it, really…

And there were some good ideas. Like, I mean, the most successful thing that we did, was, I think, 'The Black and White Show', which was... well, there was one very simple device, which was that Paddy Delaney, the club bouncer, and Ray McFall, who owned it at the time, had these sort of quasi-military uniforms, and as people were going in, they were stopping each person separately, and they were putting a black spot on the forehead of every second person. So when you got down in the Cavern, you were automatically either among whites or blacks, you know.

DB: Instant segregation...

AH: Yeah. And it was quite an uneasy feeling, cos, you know, you go with your girlfriend or something, and you're separated. And so eventually it just filled up with the black ones and the white ones. And then what happened was, as we were doing songs or poems or whatever, we had these volunteers who were building up this wall of empty detergent packets and cardboard boxes. So eventually there was a wall between the blacks and the whites. And then at the end, the band, the Clayton Squares, did this very up-tempo and loud, inspiring sort of song... And you were encouraged to trample down the wall, and dance. So it ended up with people dancing in the ruins of this mangled heap of broken cardboard boxes.

Yeah: so I think, in a way, that that sort of political element is probably what the New York school were not doing, as far as I know. It was very self-contained, sort of art-world references, really, for them. So in that sense, I suppose, we were doing something slightly different.

Sampson & Barlow's

DB: What were the Sampson & Barlow's nights like: were those all poetry, or were those partly poetry, partly music, at that time?

AH: Yeah. There was always somebody who would get up and play guitar, usually rather badly. But there was always an element of music. Because it was a folk club called the Washhouse, and that was Tuesday to Friday or something, and then we discovered that we could have it on Monday nights, free of charge if they could open up the bar and sell ale. So, I think, almost, right along, something of the folk club sort of ethos, which is a come-all-ye thing – that anybody can stand up and sing a song – I think that that almost immediately entered into what we were doing. So, apart from

the advertised attractions, there were always voices from the audi-
ence, and things, right from day one, really, as I remember. And I
used to do, you know, very silly things, like audience participation.
I'd get everybody to write one word or one line on a piece of paper,
and collect it in the interval, and people read it out after the interval,
and things like that.

DB: In the 1960s you mentioned that Roger McGough and Brian
Patten and yourself were wanting to change the mid-Atlantic thing.
What other local poets did you particularly rate at that time?

AH: I think there was just – Yeah, I mean, there were other people at
Sampson & Barlow's. There were other people doing things at the
time, that are now just forgotten. I mean, it's just one of those many
things. So I suppose that this guy, Weinblatt, I was talking about…

DB: Mike Weinblatt.

AH: Yeah. And a lot of other people, who just would stand up and do
it. And Mike Evans, I suppose. I mean, he was a very important man
with me. Yeah, there were people who were sort of continuing the tra-
dition, as it were, and consciously inspired by what we were doing,
albeit a bit younger.

The Henri, McGough and Patten Poems on Shared Themes

DB: From the 1960s' poems by you and Roger McGough and Brian
Patten, there are various themes that come out: as well as the Batman
ones, there's 'Galactic Lovepoem', which sits beside Patten's poem
'The Astronaut'. Then there's a series of death poems – not that every
poet doesn't write about death anyway. Your own 'Great War Poems'
sit alongside 'A Square Dance' and 'On Picnics', and 'Sleep Now'.
Then there's 'Don't Worry, Everything's Going To Be All Right', and
'For You Everything's Going To Be All Right'. And there are the three
Meat poems. Was there actually a conscious decision to write poems
on the same subjects?

AH: Batman, definitely. We actually did a Batman night in Sampson
& Barlow's. The television version had just come out, and we were all
entranced. We watched every episode. And all that kind of POW!
WHAM! And it was just… Well, you must know it yourself: if you run
weekly things, eventually you just run out; and you go, I can't just do
the same old thing again. So eventually you have a night when you
have a shared theme. And we did Batman as that, actually. So that
was, as it were, the world premiere of 'Batpoem', 'Goodbat Nightman'

and 'Where Are You Now, Batman?' They were all on the same night, in fact. So that was a very consciously shared theme.

Other than that, I think they were just things that were around in the atmosphere, really. Except, I think, the 'Great War Poems'. I know there was some significant anniversary [summer 1964 marked the 50th anniversary of the outbreak of the First World War]; and I remember, the colour supplements had just started to come out, and there was a wonderful colour essay on the old battlefields; and all these very poignant images of, you know, shoes that were still in the mud, and all that. And I think that, certainly mine, the 'Great War Poems', and I think Roger's 'A Square Dance', were actually for an occasion.

DB: Then there's the three Meat poems, like your own 'Meat Poem', Roger McGough's 'There Was A Knock On The Door. It Was The Meat'; and Brian Patten's 'Meat'. Did that come from a theme being set, or was that chance?

AH: No. That's very much chance, really. And they were later, anyway. I remember the occasion for 'There Was A Knock On The Door. It Was The Meat', and that was when we were touring Germany, me and Roger, and we were in a restaurant in Munich. And, as you do, we said we'd like to eat something that's local. And they said, I would recommend this; and it was called *Schlachtplatte*. And we said, What is it? And they said, Roughly translated, it means, 'something freshly slaughtered.' And I remember Roger saying, 'I'll have one of those with chips.'

Plastic Daffodils

DB: Let's talk plastic daffodils. As well as plants being ubiquitous in your poetry, there are the imitation plants, especially plastic daffodils, turning up from very early on. What kicked that off?

AH: Oddly enough, I remembered exactly what happened, the other day, actually. I was doing this series of paintings called *Liverpool 8*. And I realised – I was under the influence of Rauschenberg and things – I couldn't find a method of securing greenery to a picture. If I did, then it would just die. So I thought: plastic flowers. And at that time, plastic daffodils were given away free if you purchased a packet of Omo. So I had a supply of these, and I wanted some more. So I went along to Lewis's, where they had a big counter full of artificial flowers, and I said, 'Can I have some daffodils, please?' and she said, 'You can't –

they're out of season.' And I just thought: that's the most incredible thing. And that's a paradox if ever there was one: the idea that you could actually only buy them when they were in season; and as soon as they were out of season, they'd put them away somewhere. So that was the origin of that one.

DB: And there's artificial lilies-of-the-valley, as well...

AH: Yeah. That was me and Heather Holden, really. That was just a private symbol, really. I always have liked lily-of-the-valley. And I think the perfume, the smell of lily-of-the-valley is the most evocative thing I know, really. And I think it was just a private thing that lovers do: you know, when you have little symbols that don't mean anything to other people, but they mean something to you. So in a way it's almost the opposite of the plastic daffodils. It was a sort of substitute for the real thing, really, I suppose. And that was because the real thing, the *muguets des bois*, the lilies-of-the-valley don't actually last very long, do they? They sort of bloom... And I also like them, I think, because they bloom in unlikely places, like my backyard, for instance, and they grow like wildfire there; and almost nothing else does. So it always seemed to me that in some sense it was a poetic sort of image, that this lovely thing is languishing in these backyards, and these dismal sort of places. So it was a bit of that as well, I think, as well as just a private symbolism of the poet.

'Mrs Albion...', 'Without You' and 'I Want To Paint'

DB: One of my favourite early ones of yours is 'Mrs Albion You've Got A Lovely Daughter'. Phil Bowen mentions in his book that it was actually written on Albion Street. How did that poem come to be written?

AH: Because Allen Ginsberg was in Liverpool, and he'd got an obsession about William Blake, and in fact the late Arthur Ballard, my then employer, head of department at the art school, was giving us – was giving Allen, really – a tour around Liverpool, and we went to St George's, Everton, which is the cast iron church, and on the way out, Allen suddenly noticed this street called Albion Street; and of course he was entranced, because it was a Blakeian sort of sign. So that was one strand of that poem, which was just this chance occurrence of the Albion Street name, as we were walking through Everton. And then the other obvious thing, the pop song, you know, 'Mrs Brown You've Got A Lovely Daughter'. It was in the top 20, I think. The ghastly

Herman's Hermits. So there was that. And then… So I had the idea of the Daughter of Albion; and then when I got back, and having – Ginsberg having gone home, whatever, I actually recognised in Blake that there were these mythological giants, that the Daughters of Albion were actually the four major rivers of the country. The Thames… and I imagined one of them being the Mersey.

DB: In the poem itself, the 'most lovely daughter' is actually Liverpool, isn't it?

AH: Yeah. So when that first image came to me… about the Daughter of Albion dangling her landing stage in the water, it was a direct reference to William Blake. So on the one hand, it's a joke: it's about Herman's Hermits and so on; it's also about Liverpool girls, an admiring poem about the way they carry on, really, I suppose. And also it's got this major subtext, if you look for it, about Blake. It says '"Billy Blake is fab" written on a wall in Mathew Street.' You know, it's only there if you look for it. The poem doesn't depend on the reference to Blake, really.

DB: It strikes me that it's a poem that looks to the extraordinary within the ordinary, which is part of what Blake was about.

AH: Yes, I think that's a fair comment. It is.

DB: Another two early poems that stood out for me: one we've already talked about, 'I Want To Paint'; another one is 'Without You', which has got your use of paradox again, all the way through it…

AH: I suppose in a way it was a sort of mannerism almost; but I only stopped doing it when I realised I had imitators who were doing it as well… In a sense it was a different person, a different girl, because it was actually about a real girl, you know. It was about Heather Holden and my relationship with her. And so in that sense it was very much opposite from 'I Want To Paint', although she came into that as well. But, yeah. It is an idea of paradox that runs all the way through it, I suppose. And it's just a literary conceit, really, I suppose. But at the time, it was very liberating. And then eventually, towards the end of the 1960s, I found it… as I say, there were imitation Adrian Henri poems appearing in magazines, and they all did this paradox thing. And so I finally dropped it, I suppose. And then, I was me-writing-when-I-was-in-a-band; and then when I stopped doing that, I did a book called *Autobiography*, which was a quite different kettle of fish, and you know, I hope there was no taste of the old Adrian Henri in that. Yeah, it was a major secondary direction, really, I think, to do that.

DB: In 'Without You' and in 'I Want To Paint', both of those use that repetitive structure, which builds into a flight, or crescendo…

AH: Well, I got it from Apollinaire, via Allen Ginsberg. I think that was the route it went. Anyway, I'd read Apollinaire a lot, and I liked it very much; and a lot of his had that repetitive framework. And then, I was aware of Ginsberg and Corso doing the same thing, only in different ways. And then it was my version of their version of Apollinaire, really, I suppose, that I was doing. And again, it was an immensely satisfying experience, for a bit, until you were relying on it, you know. But I think that when they work, those poems, they're actually not quite the expected thing, so there's always something in them that's slightly askew, so that you get tragic and funny all sort of mixed up.

O'Connor's and the Liverpool Scene

DB: What were the differences between the Sampson & Barlow's scene and the later O'Connor's scene?

AH: Well, the later O'Connor's scene was… By then we were in fact notionally a band, called Liverpool Scene, which included people like Mike Hart, Mike Evans…

DB: Had the band already formed when the O'Connor's nights started?

AH: It was almost coincidental, really. When the landlord asked us, I think there'd been some kind of… we couldn't do the Everyman any more, for various reasons, and the landlord of O'Connor's, Jimmy Moore, said how about us using the upstairs once a week, and I think either the band was just forming or was about to be formed. So there was always a deliberate musical element in it. And a lot of the things that we later did on stage, or on record, were actually first tried out in O'Connor's. I mean, we did a musical version of 'The Entry Of Christ Into Liverpool', for example, which we did originally just with the drummer and me at first. And then it was, I think Andy Roberts, who had an idea for doing something, and then it was so-and-so. So it sort of accumulated; it started as one, then two people, and ended up as six people.

DB: On the album, that's a full band thing. Is that roughly the version you were playing live, by the end of those nights?

AH: Yeah. It was very much a try-out place for anything, really, that we happened to want to do; and the audience were incredibly patient and long-suffering.

DB: You imply that things didn't always go smoothly.

AH: Oh yeah. Oh yeah. But at the time it was all right.

DB: Were there any other regular poets doing stuff at O'Connor's?

AH: Apart from Mike Evans, there was Sid Hoddes, I think, who's still around. There were always others than just the Liverpool Scene people. And then we'd get occasional guests as and when: Christopher Logue one night, and Adrian Mitchell another night. Mostly, other poetic friends, really.

Ubu and the Liverpool Scene

DB: Kustow reckoned that in your use of Père Ubu, there was actually a kind of identification going on...

AH: I know what he's saying, yeah. I mean, it's almost like a sort of me-substitute, really, 'cos I was way fat, and I suppose quite badly behaved, really, in my time. And I think in a way, it's that Ubu is a sort of incarnation of that thing: you know, he's fat and he's gross, and he's cowardly; and he's all those things you wouldn't want to be, really; except that he's a survivor in some way. So in all the things, you know, he's just lost the throne of Poland, and he's just upset with life, and he's going on to Denmark to try again in Denmark. It's all that, and I think that that's the thing that I sort of identify with in him, really.

Alfred Jarry is one of my cultural heroes, anyway. I mean, not just Ubu... I was thinking just the other day: he's got a wonderful poem about a lobster that falls in love with a tin of corned beef, and it actually has, the quote in English is, 'Boneless and economical', and that's on the wrapper, presumably. But it's... That's a mad idea, a lobster falling in love with a tin of corned beef. And lots and lots of his work was inspirational, I suppose, in a bizarre sort of way.

DB: As well as being a character of immense greed, Ubu is also someone who plays on paradox all the time.

AH: Yeah, again, it is Ubuesque, I suppose. Because the famous thing where in one of the plays, he has his conscience in a suitcase, and every so often he consults it, and he always does exactly the opposite of what it says. So, yeah, I suppose paradox is one of my things really.

DB: Something else that Mike Kustow points out is that in your portrayals of Ubu – and I can see this in the paintings but also in your poetry – he at times becomes a rather sad and lost character.

AH: Yeah, I think it was always inside of me, you know. It was just, because I've always been an apparent extrovert, it's always been the side you didn't show, really. And, yeah, I've done some pretty extrovert things in my life, I suppose. And… I mean, it's always been there, and it's quite perceptive of Kustow to spot it, really, that underneath the apparent façade, there's a someone else… He actually says it about my *Ubu On Rhyl Sands,* where he says he looks lost and lonely, or something; and I suppose there is that sense of loneliness that is in the writing, but you have to look for it, really; and it's there if you want to find it.

DB: Moving on briefly to complete trivia, I noticed that somewhere in Phil Bowen it mentions that you were regularly drinking ten pints a night. Is that statistic true?

AH: Yeah. Yeah. Oh yeah. When I was in a band, when I was in Liverpool Scene, I used to really put it away, you know: it was a regular ten pints a night, really. And the other thing was that I was 17 or 18 stone, and I was jumping off stages and generally carrying on. And what happened is, you know, you put a strain on your system: so I had a minor heart attack in 1970, and that changed my life in a lot of ways, really.

The manager of the Liverpool Scene, Sandy Robertson, had already fixed me and Andy Roberts to start another group, and get a record contract and things. And indeed, Roberts was rehearsing some people; and I just said, I don't want to do it any more, you know. It was a commitment that I'd made at some sacrifice to the other things I did, because I loved the idea of doing poetry onstage, and doing it in front of an audience, basically a rock'n'roll audience, not a poetry audience at all; and I loved it. I think some of the happiest times in my life were when things were going well with that. I think the climax really, in many ways, was the Isle of Wight Festival in 1969; and we played to about 250,000 people, and it worked, you know. They actually listened. I mean, somebody who was in the crowd, later said, you could have heard a pin drop when you were doing the poems and things.

And I wouldn't have changed that for anything really. But when I had to make another decision, I thought, Am I going to go through this whole experience again, you know, do another three years on the road before I get back to where I went? And it didn't seem worth it, so I said, No, I'm not going to do it, and I'll just sort of freelance, and get money from whatever I'm doing. So in a way, that's a thing that didn't happen.

The other thing that happened, or didn't happen, was that a man from another record company had been keeping an eye on what we were doing: Tony Stratton-Smith, from Charisma Records. I met him some time later, and he said, You know, it was remarkable, because I was going to make a substantial offer to buy you out from your management and record contract, and you would all have done very well out of it; and I think that morning or as he was making up his mind, he opened the newspaper and it said 'Liverpool Scene Splits'. So that was that. That was my one chance of being a real rock'n'roll star gone.

Wish You Were Here

DB: In *Wish You Were Here,* two of the poems I particularly liked were set in particular streets: 'Honeysuckle' and 'Suburban Landscape with Figures'. In 'Honeysuckle' you've got this tale of love which ends with the sad image of the dying honeysuckle. Could you tell me what went into the writing of that one?

AH: Well it's a true story actually. It's embroidered, but it is just me, fancying the wife of a near neighbour, and in that strange way that you do, I think we both knew about it. But for various reasons – and one very obvious one, which was her husband – it never happened really. It sort of almost happened. And as you say, the ending is the honeysuckle dying. I think what I like about it is not just that it's an urban romance, but I think it has almost a fairytale quality. I think it's all numbers, you know: fourteen years, and then after seven years she planted honeysuckle at the door, so it's got a sort of almost fairytale quality which I really like, actually. But it is in essence a true story, albeit a rather sad one.

DB: In 'Suburban Landscape with Figures', you've got this very ordinary scene at first, and then this startling, gruesome background. How did that come to be written?

AH: That's Dennis Nilsen. I had a major project – I think they'd just caught Peter Sutcliffe, and then there was Nielsen, and then there was something else. And I gathered lots of press coverage about it, because like most of the population – they won't admit to it – I'm fascinated by killers and what makes them tick, and things. So I was going to have a long ambitious poem that would somehow encapsulate all these people; and what it turned out to be was just one, and that was Dennis Nilsen. And it's the idea of somebody leading this quiet, suburban life; and unknown to almost everyone, except his victims, doing the most bizarre and awful things. So it's sort of like, what goes on behind the façade of ordinariness, I suppose.

DB: Yeah. That contradicts the FACE OF EVIL approach that the tabloids have.

AH: Yeah, 'cos he didn't seem an evil person, and he was mild-mannered. He was in an office, wasn't he: he worked in some sort of government department, and he was always the one who remembered birthdays and things. And it just seemed so – and I read, as well, a good book about him [*Killing for Company* by Brian Masters]; and one of the things that was startling was that the only episode in his life that actually seemed to have an impression upon him at all was seeing his grandfather in his coffin.

Not Fade Away

DB: Moving to *Not Fade Away:* you must have been very pleased with that as a collection, and the response to it.

AH: Yeah. A lot of people said it's the best one yet, and things. Which is nice, because I always get, 'You're the sixties poet, aren't you.' They only want to talk about my old work; so the idea that people were actually concentrating on the new work was very complimentary really.

DB: Two of the poems I really like in that are both elegies, but they're very different poems. One, the Sam Walsh one, 'A Portrait of the Artist': that one's full of regret and dreams, some of them lost, and that...

AH: Yeah. Sam was very close to me, although we had our differences. And there was a lot of regret when he died, basically because he had too much talent that he wasn't using, really. His painting had gone off. His drawing was still there; but then, you know, he just self-destructed, really. That's all you can say.

DB: On drink...

AH: Yeah. And so, I suppose, yeah, it's an elegy for him really; but as you say, it's also about lost dreams as well. I was dreaming what I thought Sam might have dreamt; but on the other hand it was also me as well, that sense of wanting to do something large and make a bold statement, and really try to change people's perceptions, or something. And that wasn't just common to me and Sam; it's a lot of artists, really, who feel that in various ways. So in some sense it is an elegy for Sam, but it's also an elegy as well for lost hopes.

DB: The other elegy that leapt out is very different in tone. 'Blue for Slim' has a nice lightness at the same time as being sad…

AH: I met Slim Gaillard in the Chelsea Arts Club, about ten years ago, maybe. 'Cos he was living in England. I used to have some of those nonsense records of his, when I was a teenager… And here was the guy who was, in a way, another hero. You know there's a reference to him in *On The Road,* and things. The incredible Dadaist sort of language that he used: 'Cement mixer, puttee puttee,' you know. And, of course, from being literally a slim young man, he was quite hefty I suppose, and had got a great sort of patriarchal beard. But he would go into the club, the Chelsea Arts Club, and he would wander to the piano, and the next thing, he'd just start doing all this stuff, you know. And I got to know him quite well, and he came to a poetry reading of mine, and I was really, you know, 'Gosh, *he's* come to hear *me*,' not the… and he really liked it. And it was just… I don't know; I can't say he was a friend, but he was a hero-cum-acquaintance, I suppose you might say. So it wasn't like the Elvis poem, which was just about fame, and all that thing. It's a slightly more private one than that, because I actually did know him.

DB: In *Not Fade Away,* you continue with some very sensual use of plants and vegetation, in 'Winter Garden', and in the most extreme case, in 'Thicket'. Plants have always been very important in your poetry, and in that very sensual way sometimes…

AH: Yeah. I think, if you go to the exhibition, you see where it comes from. I mean, the first room of the exhibition is almost entirely urban, and where there's a reference to nature at all, it's plastic daffodils.

On the other hand, in the early 1970s, I was… It was a kind of epiphany, really. I was walking my friend's dog along this hedge in Much Wenlock in Shropshire, and I suddenly thought: I want to paint the hedge. And what I ended up doing, and it's in the exhibition, was a 14-foot hedge in three panels, and just trying to put everything that I knew about in. I didn't know about flowers, 'cos I was an urban lad, you know; I wasn't at all a country boy, so it was rather laboriously learned at first, all those plants, you know, meadowsweet – I wouldn't have known a meadowsweet if it came up and bit me, really, until I started writing those things, doing those paintings, and starting to write about them; and in some sense they've never gone away really, even when I don't actually do hedges and whatever any more. It's always been an element now in the poetry.

DB: It was always there in the background... You've always been very particular in the names of plants you refer to.

AH: Yeah. I suppose it's what I appreciate with other people too; you know, that what I really like is not just that it's a flower, but it's a particular plant or particular animal, or flower or whatever it is. And naming, I think, is one of the things that poetry is very good at, in a way. By naming something, you sort of, appropriate it. I think that's very important, really, in a funny sort of way.

It's almost like a background activity that you're not really conscious of. But you know, I've always kept notebooks, and they're full of names of things and names of places and... signs in shop windows. You know: the names of things. And once I've got that, I can't lose it. Once I've got it, it might not end up in a picture or a poem, but I've got it there somewhere. It's a sort of thirst for information really.

DB: Among your poems, what few pieces are you most proud of?

AH: I don't know.

DB: It's a terrible question, I know.

AH: It is, actually, yeah. Well, a lot of the ones that you've talked about have been my favourite ones, anyway, as it happens. I think, this one called 'Morning Song', that begins, 'Of meat and flowers I sing' – not because of the poem itself, but because it then led to a big painting of meat and flowers that I did, which I won a painting prize for. So in a way it was a sort of two-stage thing: it was a poem before it was a painting, but I wouldn't have had the idea for the painting if it wasn't for the poem. So there are things like that... Umm...

DB: Yeah, it was a grossly unfair question...

AH: Yeah.

Strokes, Convalescence and Poetry

DB: I gather you're finding it still very difficult after your strokes...

AH: Yeah, it's sort of one step forward and sometimes two steps back, you know. Most weeks you get an improvement, and then every so often you get a setback, so you have to start again, really. The main thing it's left me with is an inability to write, actually. It's amazing because, painting – I mean, I've done a lot of drawing and stuff, and pastels and things in the hospital and elsewhere, and that's been fine, you know; but there's something about... it's like acute dyslexia, really. So I literally can't see words. So if I read, right, I just read, and that goes through my head, and that's fine. It's only if you say to me 'Read that,' that I would maybe start jumping words and things; and then when it gets to writing down anything, [holds up hand] I've literally got almost no capacity to actually write.

So I've been actually doing some poems – I started about a fortnight ago – into a tape recorder, and Catherine's been transcribing them; so that's the first one since the stroke, in fact. It's quite laborious, actually. I mean, the idea of you speaking into a tape recorder, and then somebody else trying to make sense of what you're trying to say and transcribe it for you: it's a bit of a labour of love.

But I've just done a commissioned thing for my old university, and I've got a couple of other things, and I've now got an idea for... when the illness struck, I was halfway through doing a collection of poems for children...

DB: Was it March that you had the stroke?

AH: February last, about the 14th or 15th of February. But before that, I had a by-pass operation, and then before that I had a heart attack. You know, I mean, it goes on. So poor old Catherine's been coping with all that, basically.

The Day of the Dead, Hope Street, and the Shadow Person

DB: You were working on *The Day of the Dead, Hope Street,* before that. Tell me about that book project...

AH: Well, it's still an unpublished manuscript at the moment. I mean it's just doing the rounds at the moment. To be honest, one or two people looked at it, and I don't know whether it's really good enough or not. But 'The Day of the Dead...', the actual poem that goes with the work, is fine, I think; and there are a couple of other things that I really like. I think always, with a collection, it's sort of like you're not quite sure whether they're all right, or whether they're just all right but not quite good enough to stand publication.

DB: Did you say that that's going out to publishers already?

AH: Yeah.

DB: Oh right. 'Cos I wasn't quite sure if it was actually finished or not.

AH: Put it this way: it was put together, well, just before this thing started; so it was about a year ago, and I sent it to my agent; and Bloodaxe, who did the last one, for some reason didn't want to do this one. So they've been sort of, hawking it round. So I don't know. I mean maybe I'll rewrite it, or rethink it, or something. I mean, I've shown the manuscript to Willy and Carol Ann and people, and they say... I mean, they're very complimentary, but that may just... you know. It's helpful to have outside opinion; but it's nothing like knowing that it's fine and it's OK and it's good with you. I know the last two poems – Did you see the Liverpool *Ambit*?[5]

DB: Oh yeah.

AH: Because the two ones I did which were the last before I went into hospital were actually, I think, two of the things that I'm most proud of, really.

DB: There was the aubade... ['Aubade, Ward E']

AH: Mm, that's right. Yeah, I really liked that. I just thought that there was something in those that... I suppose it's the situation, really. Being in that place and seeing all the suffering around you, does something... It's a very different experience from, you know, the 'I am a poet, I'm suffering.' It's a quite different sort of situation really. You know, somebody dies in the next bed to you, and it just happens, you know. It alters your whole perspective on life, really. And then almost dying myself, really... And in a way, I haven't quite come to terms with it, in terms of actual writing.

I think it's different with painting, because it's out there; it's something that's sort of outside of yourself, really.

Although in a way I am a sort of autobiographical painter, it's only relative. I mean I couldn't imagine trying to paint myself in a hospital bed, for example. I just couldn't do that: it wouldn't be my sort of painting. Whereas, I mean, John Bellany, for example, has done a lot of hospital paintings, and they're fine. But they're just different; they're just... You know, he's him and I'm me. So, it's sort of, having to come to terms with the whole world changing around you, really, that's very different.

DB: Presumably in the poetry that you've been starting to write again recently, that'll be reflected?

AH: Yeah. I mean one's a sort of autobiographical piece, because it was just a commission. But the other two are pretty personal things really. One of them's a sort of, very anguished – well, I don't know, maybe it's not anguished, I don't know – but it's very much about being you but not you. And the clue I think is the famous saying of Rimbaud, where he says 'Je suis un autre' – 'I am not me; I am someone else.'[6] And what I've got is an odd feeling that inside of me there's a second person. I mean, I know it's not, I know he's not, and I know that it can only be me; but it doesn't feel like me, so it's this idea of otherness, the idea of, you know, I am not me, I'm some other kind of person, who is… almost like – it's a bit like *The Invasion of the Body Snatchers,* you know: that someone's taken over your personality. Occasionally a feeling almost like that.

DB: How would you describe the other that you're talking about, there?

AH: Well, that's the trouble, because it's me. It's just me-different, that's all. It intrudes on my thoughts, very often. I can be writing or just thinking about something or reading something, and suddenly this thing obtrudes that is not me in the sense that, it's not conscious volition; it's just there. And often it's quite maddening sort of things, like old songs from my childhood, bits of things I learned at school; all sorts of things, but it isn't conscious, in the sense that I can't really control it.

DB: This is purely over the last year, did you say?

AH: Yeah. Well, I suppose it arose as I've become more and more conscious of what has happened to me, really, because obviously, when I was just lying in a hospital bed and not moving, as you're lying there and you haven't got any sort of way of expressing yourself, the only thought that comes out is the thought that comes out – just the thought; whereas as I'm getting better and moving around and doing things, I can think clearly about some things, but at the same time this little voice at the back is saying something else, you know, so it's like there's two people talking. I mean, one's got a louder voice than the other now. Before, it was like a dialogue; and now it's sort of like a background noise, but it's still there. I'm still conscious of the fact that there is this other, sort of, shadow person that is around.

> This is not my face
> This owlish staring
> pair of eyes
> This is not my face…
>
> This is not my mind
> Someone else's mind
> Someone who knows

the same things I know
but knows them differently
This constant useless
barrage of information
Songs that only I could know
Songs from my childhood
Things we did at school
Forties pop songs
rise unbidden from my head...
Somewhere in the darkness
lying, abandoned, is the real me
Until then, it is just you
Je est un autre
Je suis un autre
Je suis un autre

(Excerpts from draft of 'Je suis un Autre' by permission of Adrian Henri)

Notes

1   Phil Bowen, *A Gallery To Play To: The Story of The Mersey Poets,* Exeter, Stride, 1999, p. 30.
2   Bowen, *A Gallery To Play To*, p. 33.
3   Adrian Henri, *Environments and Happenings*, London, Thames & Hudson, 1974, p. 117.
4   Edward Lucie-Smith, *The Liverpool Scene*, London, Donald Carroll, 1967.
5   *Ambit* 158, 1999, a special edition of the poetry magazine devoted to Liverpool.
6   'That's a misquote though,' Catherine Marcangeli points out during a follow-up interview. 'The quote is "Je est un autre". You know, "I is another", as opposed to "I am another".'

An Interview with Brian Patten

Stephen Wade

I spoke to Brian Patten in London; the interview had been arranged in something of a rush, as he had a new book out that week and his schedule was hectic. But there we were, in a quiet room at last, and time to bring his Liverpool phase back to mind. In some ways, the phrase 'Liverpool poet' is a suit that doesn't fit comfortably any more in Patten's case. He seems to have outreached, but certainly not abandoned his writing about his origins and early years; quite the contrary. It becomes more and more obvious that with Patten, as with so many poets, the formative years are always there, even if their presence is a little spectral and blurred. In fact, some quite startling things came from the interview in this regard. For instance, the cultural significance of his achievements in the mid-1960s are perhaps not clear to him yet. His part in the establishment of an aesthetic and a specific imaginative nexus for the Mersey Sound and its poetry did not seem to be significant to him. He rarely thinks about the old times, and certainly doesn't look back with soft-centred nostalgia to that period of work on the *Bootle Times* and the beginnings of his writing with the magazine *Underdog*.

His objective stance became clear as the talk progressed. But Liverpool is clearly still a mental, creative landscape for him; it is perhaps emblematic of a phase of consciousness, mixing uneasily the schoolboy and the teenager, and various sorts of rebellion. In this, Patten's life is remarkably bohemian, and at times akin to Arthur Rimbaud's (one of his first poetic stylistic models) in the sense of a purposeful, almost educative drifting into experience 'further than at home, where small experience grows' as Shakespeare puts it.

In the interview, I struggled to keep Liverpool as the centre, as there had been so much else. But Linda Cookson's book on Patten[1] provided some cues. He was keen to explore the early years, but reluctant to see anything there that might, in future, identify the city and the period as a British Frisco City Lights/Ginsberg relative. He has too much sanity, realism and propensity for calm reflection for such rhetoric.

SW: Brian, how far is the Liverpool childhood behind you – in an imaginative sense?

BP: Nothing is that simple. The latest book has been totally about my childhood. It's all there. All still part of me. Does it matter to me – is that what you're asking?

SW: Is it 'with' you?

BP: It's with me in the sense that my childhood made me what I am now so I don't think you can separate the two.

SW: How did you become a poet?

BP: I maybe first realised I could write when I wrote a poem to get off the cross-country run at school. I'd say, 'I'll write you a poem sir.' And that's what I'd do.

SW: Could we start with the image of a poet then? Did you have any figures or heroes in that respect?

BP: When you talk about the image of a poet, it was live fast, die young, wasn't it? Rimbaud's kind of lifestyle – that Romantic notion was there. It was part of it – part of any kind of youth.

SW: It stood out in the way you were marketed. Did you have any part in the early images of yourself, such as the photographs on the cover of *Little Johnny's Confession*[2] which show you looking moody and contemplative?

BP: No.

SW: Were you misrepresented in that context?

BP: No, because that kind of poetry wasn't being written really. There was a very urban poetry but it was different...

SW: Was Liverpool 8 and the whole idea (maybe as in John Cornelius's book)[3] in a way mythologised, or was it as important for poetry as has been claimed?

BP: I think it was. If you trace the idea you even get Ben Zephaniah, and almost anyone now – you end up in Liverpool 8. An idea, not a place in a complete sense. I think Ben married a girl from there. It was a very open atmosphere. You could wander into other people's houses and get very excited about the work you saw – showing it and sharing it – it was a small city, people didn't live very far from each other, so there would be a lot of interaction, the artists and the poets. But in a place like London you wouldn't have that kind of split. The Left Bank or certain areas of San Francisco – Liverpool 8 was like that.

SW: Did the media have an effect on you?

BP: I did feel very much, when I started doing readings, that it should all lock in and come together. Maybe the media made you feel that.

SW: Poetry itself, as a subject, seemed to be important?

BP: The prose poem I did – that was a kind of manifesto.

SW: Poetry as a central part of life?

BP: It's source is that.

SW: Did Liverpool at the time provide something to act against?

BP: No – not the case at all.

SW: It was a stimulating place, not a frightening one?

BP: Yes, very.

SW: Did the feeling that you had to broaden out come early?

BP: No, it just grows. I can't speak for anyone else, but all my poetry is just about what's happening – almost like a diary.

SW: You've never had a problem with that?

BP: But I recognise that the 'I' in the poem is not unique. We all go through these experiences, so the 'I' is a shared 'I', you see.

SW: I haven't asked you yet about that particular Liverpool magic that was feeding the media at the time. How do you respond to Allen Ginsberg's famous statement that 'Liverpool was the centre of human consciousness' at that time?

BP: He probably thought it was the centre of his universe because there were a lot of boy bands in tight jeans. I'm sure that's behind that.

SW: Is there a germ of truth, though, in Liverpool being that huge?

BP: It's a massive statement. He was excited by things.

SW: In 'Maud' you refer to the 'half-relationships' – was this Liverpool or all places and people?

BP: I wasn't thinking of Liverpool. It was to do with disenfranchised youth.

SW: We've not mentioned class. I felt that poetry was part of a middle-class thing when I, like you, went to a secondary modern school. When you wrote then, were you thinking of a working-class readership or audience – or did you have any sense of having an axe to grind in that way?

BP: No – but if it was working class, it came out working class – as simple as that. The audience was not necessarily a university audience. They were in jobs. So it didn't seem to enter into the consciousness really.

SW: I thought of poetry books as part of a middle-class opposition –

some way of trying to convert you. Can you identify with that? I'm thinking of you missing the cross-country run if you stayed in and wrote a poem.

BP: Well no, I mean are the middle classes really interested in poetry? Who assumes this? I'd take issue with you if you're claiming that the middle class is more interested in poetry.

SW: Fine. It's in need of research! Would you say that part of the creativity in you then, in Liverpool, was related to fear? Did you never see the place as a large, scary city in which your family problems and so on mixed to provoke your imagination?

BP: The family life – that could have happened anywhere. I was in early street gangs and stuff. I grew up with my mother and grandmother. But that seems normal.

SW: I was led to see 'the arts' as marginalised at school. Were you?

BP: Nobody did the arts as it were – in the catchment area of our school nobody did it.

SW: Do you see poetry in any radically different way now?

BP: One can come up with quite glib definitions of it really. I mean, I'm more likely to say now that poetry reminds us of what we forgot we knew. But it changes. Books like *Armada*[4] and *Little Johnny's Confession* are a million miles apart. Things do change. People die, cancers creep… your attitude changes.

SW: Do you still agree with your early statements about poetry?

BP: Yes, but it's never really concerned the three of us deeply. We don't go around making statements. Then, we worked differently – I mean compared with the route of a professional in poetry – writing reviews and so on.

SW: There was no literary culture around the poems?

BP: No – just the poems. Say, something like *Underdog* – there are no articles or reviews of poetry in there.

SW: Was the title your invention?

BP: Yes.

SW: I'd like to ask you about *Underdog*. Are you aware just how important these early editions will be in years to come?

BP: No. I worked with another man – I've lost touch with him – it was when I was the cub reporter. I used the typewriter and then we had this copier for the photos… [At this point, we look at some early issues of *Underdog*. There are illustrations, an image of McGough, contributions from Americans and from lesser-known contemporaries in Liverpool. All the indications are that it is different from a student writing magazine. Everything is more direct, less pretentious, and poetry is assumed to be important simply for its being, not its claims of significance.]

SW: So you did most of it yourself?

BP: Yes, put it together, saw to the circulation, all that.

SW: Why didn't you treat Liverpool in a documentary way? I mean it was the fashion then to make [one's] writing closer to journalism if you were dealing with poorer folk or if you were being 'regional'.

BP: Because we weren't journalists.

SW: OK. Now, what would be a typical session at Streate's or a similar place?

BP: Well, everybody did their thing. You had songs and poems, and Roger did these dialogues. Adrian would do the visual stuff…

SW: Was it really a bohemian atmosphere?

BP: You could say that in a way…

SW: What about your own life at this point? I'm intrigued by the fact that you lived in France and Ireland at times.

BP: I was the first pavement poet in France. I met this girl… she would translate the poems, then I'd chalk them on the pavements… and it paid my food and bed bills.

SW: I've noticed that French writing was important to both yourself and to Roger McGough, who taught some French at one time…

BP: Yes, Rimbaud, Verlaine… I read this book. [Brian showed me the dog-eared copy of a 1960s poetry anthology on a bookshelf.]

SW: What are your thoughts on Liverpool in the 1960s – I mean if you had to sum up its nature, with hindsight?

BP: I remember very much, in my youth after the Second World War, the street singers. They were old men to me but they were really young men. They had been blinded or de-limbed in one way or another. They would be in the streets singing 'If I Were a Blackbird' and various songs… Then they were forced off the streets and into the alleyways. Then you would go down the alleyways and give them a threepenny bit or sixpence. And I suppose these early street singers sum Liverpool up. Rainy days and the grey streets by the gasworks where ex-servicemen were thrown up, and singing in the streets – they would sing a very sad Irish song…

SW: Is there a Liverpool temperament, as writers often claim when they talk about Scouse wit and so on?

BP: I don't know.

SW: Brian, thank you for your time.

Notes

1 Linda Cookson, *Brian Patten*, Plymouth, Northcote House, 1997.
2 Brian Patten, *Little Johnny's Confession*, London, George Allen and Unwin, 1967.
3 John Cornelius, *Liverpool 8*, London, John Murray, 1982; reprinted Liverpool, Liverpool University Press, 2001.
4 Brian Patten, *Armada*, London, HarperCollins, 1996.

AUTOBIOGRAPHIES/
SOCIAL HISTORIES

4

Open Floor!
Live Poetry Nights in Liverpool, 1967–2001

David Bateman

Background

Open-floor nights are those sessions, usually in the back rooms or base-
ment bars of pubs, at which anyone can get up and have their five min-
utes performing their poetry, music, comedy, or whatever it is they think
they can do. If the organisers have some money to invest they may book
in a known performer as a headline act; but usually the organisers are
volunteers doing it for love and running the events on a shoestring, and
always it goes without saying that most of the participants aren't
famous and never will be. On the other hand, these sessions are where
most poets begin their performance careers, and are the spawning
grounds for bigger things.

Any regular session survives and thrives partly on its own sense of
community and partly on a sort of community reputation, which is
almost entirely separate from the mainstream of literature and of other
arts. Like little magazines, these sessions come and go with sometimes
alarming frequency. This essay is a somewhat personal attempt to track
the continuity of regular poetry sessions in Liverpool, beginning where
most examinations of Liverpool poetry end: the disappearance (whether
permanent or simply on tour) of Adrian Henri, Roger McGough and
Brian Patten.

Liverpool city centre is a compact area, a little over one square mile in
size, and nearly all the events I'm talking about take place in this area,
bounded by the lines of Great Crosshall Street and New Islington to the
north, Smithdown Lane to the east, Upper Parliament Street to the
south and the River Mersey to the west. That's pages 66 and 67 of your
Liverpool A–Z: the spread it falls open at.

By Word Of Mouth

Though I'd been writing poetry for six years, the first time I ever read any poems in public was one Saturday night in September 1980, in between the folk songs at Oily Joe's Folk Club. This was in the back room of the Hare and Hounds pub on Commutation Row, whose single row of buildings sat on the crest above William Brown Street. I'd found out about the weekly sing-around because I went to the same speech therapy group as the emcee, which says something both about the nature of the folk club and also why I'd never read out any poetry before. There were English songs, mostly jokey and mostly about sex, animals or both, and Irish songs which tended to speak favourably of the Sinn Féin boy with his orange, white and green. And as I lived only 400 yards away, there was also often poetry from then on. The back room was tiny and cramped and the paper was peeling off the walls but no one especially minded; the singing ranged from professional to the truly awful, and everyone drank quite a lot and had a good time.

I'd also heard of a monthly poetry night called 'By Word Of Mouth', and in November that year I searched along the dark and narrow Harrington Street – near Castle Street in the financial quarter of the city centre – for a pub called the Why Not? The gathering was in the basement, and I remember that on that first occasion one of my main feelings was of sheer relief that it didn't turn out to be some horribly stuffy and staid event where I'd stand out like a sore thumb and get bored senseless. Keith Whitelaw, Kevin McCann and Hayley Fox were among the younger poets reading, and they included some fairly vigorous material. Hayley Fox even wrote me a poem on the spot, and afterwards someone, I think Sid Hoddes, drove us up to the Everyman Bistro on Hope Street, where we drank until we were drunk. About three weeks after that Hayley vanished off the scene briefly for legal reasons; but it was clear from the start that there would be friends here. (The legal reasons followed the 'woolly nudes' incident in Liverpool city centre, when Hayley and others were arrested while parading wearing knitted costumes representing a naked man and woman.)

A prominent organiser was the grey-bearded and amiable Harold Hikins, a lifer-librarian (except for the Second World War) whose own poetry included many witty flights of magic realism, and touched a lot on Liverpool, inequality and the foibles of the human race, including library-users (as in his remarkable 'Dirty Book Poem'). His wife, Sylvia Hikins, was another organiser, and she also performed her poetry. They had brought out a couple of joint booklets of their poetry, and were generally key movers of that time, especially with regard to the Poetry Circus events of the 1970s and Toulouse Press. The third organiser, Sid Hoddes, was a GP who mostly wrote poetry of love and lust, and whose sharp eye for unusual metaphors gives many of his pieces a combination of wit and poignancy that sometimes parallels that of McGough. He'd performed regularly with the Liverpool Scene in the 1960s, and Scaffold had recorded a song using his lyric 'Promiscuity' (apparently considered too daring at the time, and finally released in 1998).

I knew very little of the background of By Word Of Mouth then, and how it had originated in the fall-out of the 1960s poetry scene. One night at the Why Not? while no poetry was happening, I met a very drunk man called Allan Williams who told me all about how he used to manage the Beatles, but had given them away just before they got big. I believed him so much I had to ask Harold Hikins afterwards if it was true. That's how much I knew then.

Back in the mid-1960s, the Liverpool Scene and Sid Hoddes had been performing every week at O'Connor's Tavern (known most recently as Bonkers) on Hardman Street. In 1967 when the Liverpool Scene went away on tour, Sid, along with Dave Calder and Mike Hart (sometimes of the Liverpool Scene) had kept the events going until the end of 1970. But the poets also moved on to other venues, including the Everyman basement. (The Everyman Theatre and Bistro – previously Hope Hall and its basement – had been venues for several of Adrian Henri's happenings, and would become a regular poetry venue again for Henri's Hope Street Poets in 1978.)

In 1967 three of the O'Connor's poets, Sid Hoddes, Harold Hikins and Jim Blackburn, set up By Word Of Mouth, a regular poetry night at Sampson & Barlow's on London Road. This had been the 1963 venue of the jazz nights, and then (from December on) 'humour and poetry' nights, at which Brian Patten had made such a strong impression along with Roger McGough and Adrian Henri.

The new series of poetry nights at Sampson & Barlow's was eventually ended by a falling out when Jim Blackburn tried to take sole command. The result was that Jim Blackburn took off to run the poetry nights at the Gazebo coffee bar at the bottom of Duke Street while Harold Hikins and Sid Hoddes continued together, adding David Porter to make up the triumvirate and soon moving venue to the Why Not? Here By Word Of Mouth would remain (except for a couple of to-ings and fro-ings) until the end of 1984.

Other Stories

In 1981 I began to become aware of various one-off poetry and music events, including a CND event in Dingle and a poetry and folk night in Lark Lane. It was at the latter that I first encountered Les Poissons d'Avril, a Bonzos-influenced band fronted by the poet-singer-songwriter David Symonds. Principally rhythm-and-blues and Cajun in style, while calling on their essential Englishness and all cultural points east and west, they had a kaleidoscopic quality. Relying heavily on their bizarre stage-appearance, their material ranged from satirical joke-songs to sometimes whimsical, occasionally beautiful love songs, which Dave would sing in a voice only a tremor away from a yodel.

I'd read in Sylvia Hikins's magazine *Poetry Merseyside* about a monthly poetry night in the Wirral called 'Jabberwocky'. It was started in 1970 by Diana Hendry, and was run by Peggy Poole, poetry editor and pre-senter for BBC Radio Merseyside. I went to Jabberwocky once, which took an epic bus journey to Heswall, and was desperately disappointed to spend half an hour listening to some bloke talking about how to make mediaeval musical instruments, and then another half hour listening to him and his partner playing some they'd made earlier. I felt like Dixon in *Lucky Jim,* trapped at an arty weekend at the Welches' house in the country. A few people read out some poems afterwards, but my heart had gone out of it, and I never went there again.

Meanwhile, back in Liverpool, By Word Of Mouth was happening on the last Thursday of every month. Every month except December, that is, because Christmas got in the way, and August because they had a theory that everyone was doing something else then. In fact everyone was doing sweet nothing in August, because everyone else had the same idiotic theory, and half of Liverpool was closed down for the month.

In February 1982 a new focus emerged with Joey Shields's weekly Monday music nights in the basement bar of the Casablanca on Hope Street. Joe's rock'n'roll band Vertigo featured every week, and other bands and musicians would guest, including the Big Mama Hill Blues Band. For the first couple of weeks Joe was unsure about having all these poets on, but some of them became regulars: myself, Craig Charles, Barbara Lester (previously the notorious Dame Loony), George Robinson and Big Dave Symonds all appeared with varying frequency. This kind of event, where most of the audience are there for the music more than the poetry, is a challenge for the poet: on the one hand you're reaching an entirely new audience, but on the other, there's always a big risk of dying badly. On the third hand (and there usually is one), there's the danger of underestimating the audience, trying to appeal through the lowest common denominator, and winding up as a second-rate stand-up comic. I tended to go for a 'serious sandwich' approach, each purely serious piece sandwiched by two lighter pieces, and also found myself gradually writing more new pieces geared towards live performance as well as working with music.

This scene could easily have fallen apart at the end of May, when Joe ended the series for legal reasons; but meanwhile Frank Keenan – a John Martyn influenced singer-guitarist from Glasgow – had also begun regular music and poetry nights at the Crack on Rice Street, just three stone's-throws from the Casablanca; and in April, Vincent Whose-surname-I've-forgotten had started up the Rainbow Club, a new music-poetry-comedy night on Fridays at Stanley House on Upper Parliament Street in L8. With its more relaxed, less sweaty atmosphere, this attracted the Casablanca poets and others as well. Craig Charles performed with his band there: a John Cooper Clarke clone admittedly, but with a lot of enthusiasm and a fair bit of humour. Regular poets included Keith Whitelaw, who began his poetry magazine *051* around now. His poetry was mostly delicately crafted material for the page, but he could whack out a few belters of performance pieces, like the spoof laddish poem 'Wanna Come Back To My Place?' and his bitterly poignant anti-nationalist 'National Anthem'.

In December 1983 a new series of Monday night music and poetry sessions began at the Casablanca, fronted by singer-guitarists Robbie McAllister and Gwyneth Roberts. At that time they were a duo, but by March 1984 we'd become the Probes, and we were a five-piece poetry-and-music band, including guitarist-keyboardist Dave Deakin who I'd first worked with back in 1982 at the Casablanca. The Probes played every Monday and were most often compared with the Velvet Underground, the Doors and the Fall. In short, we were rough. Not as rough as some of the audience, though: one night we were halfway through the poem 'Waiting For Beginnings' when one audience member punched another and sent him staggering backwards into me, and it was only my panther-like reflexes that saved my microphone from going where my teeth belong. Naturally, we played on like heroes. In fact we kept on playing on like heroes at the Casablanca right through until September 1984, when Robbie McAllister had a row with Casablanca staff. This resulted from Robbie's particular disability, common among guitarists, which made him unable to turn the volume knob in an anti-clockwise direction.

Regular poets on the Probes nights included Dave Symonds and John McKeown, and there'd be other musicians in too, sometimes doing stuff on their own, and sometimes working with the Probes. Martine Pack-man was a regular, and often I'd sit in the audience while she did a stint fronting the Probes, playing guitar and singing, making up the words as she went along.

When the Casablanca sessions came to their abrupt end, some of the Monday-night refugees found their way to the 'Under the Floorboards' events in the basement of Rigby's pub on Dale Street. Over the summer, Fringe '84 had organised various entertainments to run alongside Liverpool's International Garden Festival (itself one of the results of the Liverpool 8 riots of July 1981, sparked off by the arrest of poet Leroy Cooper). It was a Fringe worker, Elaine Harris, along with Rigby's man-ager Ron Astell, who first set up these nights, which provided a platform for compère-comedians the Kosher Cowboys (Dave Tracey and Andy Holme), jazz-blues duo Third Man (Elaine Harris and Pete McPartland) and the various poets and guests. Hayley Kingdom Fox was one of the first guests; Dave Symonds and I each guested a couple of times; and there'd always be a few poets among the floor spots. The acts were incredibly varied, and Elaine Harris still finds it hard to believe that she fitted the Ritchie Austin Big Band into the very confined performance area. Several of the nights in this series were absolute gems, with a wonderful hardcore of audience members whose enthusiasm encouraged the improvisatory and innovative aspects of the regular acts, and creating a genuine merging of poetry, comedy and music. Manager Ron Astell was an enthusiast for the sessions, and afterwards he'd get Third Man to rehearse their material for next time, sometimes getting Elaine to sing the same piece over and over until he was happy with it. But the intensity of his involvement was matched by the suddenness of his loss of interest, and the series ended abruptly in December. Maybe someone ought to get some grant funding and try something like it again.

Other venues came and went from 1985 to 1987. The Dolphin in Canning House, neighbouring the social security offices, made an unlikely venue for poets and bands such as Jegsy Dodd and the Sons of Harry Cross. Back in 1982, and now again in 1986, occasional series of music nights at the Everyman Bistro gave a few opportunities for poets, including Levi Tafari with the Ministry Of Love. For a while in the summer of 1987, Joey Shields ran a regular night at the Nook in Chinatown. His new rock'n'roll band, Joey Shields and the Wheels, would take its name from a line in 'Liverpool', a Poissons lyric written by Dave Symonds that noted the foibles of various local characters, Joe included.

Still by Mouth, Nil by Mouth

Through all these years, By Word Of Mouth had carried on its open-floor poetry nights, shuffling between venues in the Castle Street and Dale Street area of the city centre. Refurbishment work at the Why Not? had led to a move to the Poste House in November 1982, followed by a spell at the Pig & Whistle before a shift back to the Why Not? basement in September 1983, where it remained until the end of 1984.

As well as the Hikinses and Sid Hoddes, veterans included John Clifford and Jim Wareing (who regrettably destroyed most of his poems during an attack of the wrong sort of Christianity). Another regular was George Robinson, occasionally known to incorporate jazz into his poems. Poets moving to the fore in this period included Kevin McCann, outspoken in his debt to Matt Simpson's influence, and thoughtful in his almost imagist concision; Ken Payne, a cheerful purveyor of satire, at times wildly experimental as in his 'British Wild Flowers'; the librarian Keith Whitelaw, now running Pork Pie Press and publishing *051* magazine, which ran until 1984. Four issues of this little 20-page magazine don't seem like much at all, but they're the closest thing there is to an anthology of the By Word Of Mouth scene at that time.

Newcomers included John McKeown, Les Killip, David Symonds and Pat Riordan; also Glyn Wright, forceful in his delivery, and at that time most striking in his harsh nature poetry: his poem 'The Nature Boys', published in his second book, dates from those days. Originally entitled 'Eggers', and giving a first-person account of a gang of kids stealing birds' nests, it's very much a rural version of the kind of urban character piece that made up his first book. Another newcomer, whose poetry at that time seemed to me to consist of a sleep-inducing stream of mixed metaphors, was Barbara Murray, who eight years later would become so important in organising live poetry.

After a very brief spell (competing with a live band in the next room) at the Pen & Wig, By Word Of Mouth moved out of the downtown area and to the southwest city centre, up Mount Pleasant to the Irish Centre, where it stayed until Pat Riordan pissed on the stage and got us all thrown out. Thus in January 1986, By Word Of Mouth came to the Flying Picket.

The Flying Picket is the bar and theatre complex of the cumbersomely named Merseyside Trade Union, Community and Unemployed Resource Centre. The centre itself fronts onto Hardman Street just below Hope Street, while the Picket is set back beyond an alley and courtyard. The Tolpuddle Bar seemed like a fairly ideal poetry venue, but for various possible reasons (too many recent moves in too short a time; the Picket's invisibility from the street; the fact that MTUCURC was still fairly new and not everybody knew it; the fact that some people assumed from its venue that the poetry group was essentially political), By Word Of Mouth lost some of its occasional participants and suffered from a lack of newcomers. These problems weren't at all obvious at first, and for a while things sailed along fairly happily.

One new poet who wasn't put off was Michael Cunningham. An ex-art-teacher, now an accountant with a shy manner and depressed tone of voice, he'd only been writing poetry for a year or so when he first appeared in mid-1987; yet over the next two or three years he developed a style which, though identifiably a fusion of Liverpool and Hudders-field influences, is, as Simon Armitage puts it, 'his own and his own only.' But though there were good nights, somehow By Word Of Mouth never properly thrived at the Picket: it eventually suffered from the shortage of newcomers, and after October 1987 the event was strug-gling for numbers. Keith Whitelaw died in March 1988, only 33 years old; and Harold and Sid wound up the group in May.

The Third Room Poets

One night back in February 1988 I'd been doing a gig with Tony Cromp-ton's band Armpit at the Pink Parrot club on Duke Street. Tony (now to be encountered as street poet Tony Chestnut) was a wildly eccentric singer-songwriter-thrash-guitarist I'd first met in 1986 when Crikey It's the Cromptons and I were both gigging at the Dolphin. Anyway, at the Pink Parrot, I'd just finished my own poetry set, which had gone fine, but then I had to join in with various so-called sketches with Armpit, which degenerated into the predictable sort of totally bloody anarchic shambles with which Armpit was always so closely associated. As I came off the so-called stage, some student guy was coming up and saying he'd like to book me as support for Adrian Henri at the University Students Union. He said his name was Nick Bonnaud, the gig would be in the Mandela Bar in March, and the other support poet he was booking turned out to be George Robinson, another By Word Of Mouth veteran.

Anyway, the Union gig in the Mandela Bar happened as planned, and went fine, and Nick Bonnaud and George Robinson decided to set up a series of poetry nights. The first of the twice-monthly Monday poetry nights at the Everyman Bistro's Third Room (yet another basement) happened in April, with Adrian Henri headlining, and establishing the format of having a guest poet or two, and a number of open-floor poets. At the start the series was notable for its arguments: while Nick Bonnaud had wanted a lively performance scene that would attract students, George Robinson was keen to book poets established primarily on the printed page; and Nick felt too that he had been out-manoeuvred in George's recruitment of Rona Campbell as one of the organisers. Rona Campbell was a poet and ex-opera singer (principal soprano with the Opera Metropolitana in Caracas) with, at that time, a gentility that extended to being surprised by the amount of beer-drinking at poetry events. However, once Nick had dropped out in June, George and Rona veered closer to Nick's original views on poetry as entertainment, as well as taking on a more welcoming attitude to the poetic riff-raff. Later guests included many performance poets such as Kevin Fegan, Henry Normal, Lemn Sissay and Nick Toczek. With strictly limited numbers of open-floor spots up to 10 minutes long, local poetry came in decent healthy chunks to appreciate or to enjoy slagging off afterwards. Rona herself had her first book of poetry, *The Hedge*, published by Counterpoint in 1988; and from November 1989 she became the sole main organiser of the Third Room poetry nights. This was after the Dave Evans–Kevin Killeen–David Bateman guest night when George Robinson got barred from the Everyman Bistro for throwing beer at the poet Shirley Jones, after Shirley had thrown some wine over Andrew Bowers's libido. This event was the inspiration for Dave Evans's Ian St James Award-winning short story *A Poetry Reading On Riverside*. Incidentally, the swiftness (and licence) of the poetic grapevine is worth noticing: when Carol Ann Duffy gigged at the Third Room a month later, she mentioned hearing that women had been attacked in the Everyman.

Before getting on to answer the question, Who the hell is Andrew Bowers?, it's important to give an honourable mention to poet Mike Field and the Anarchist Centre on Seel Street. Beginning on May Day 1988, there were a number of poetry and music nights in the dim-lit cushiony-sprawly ground floor of what I presume was a squat, then got called a Mutual Aid Centre, and then didn't exist anymore. It's still the only poetry night I've ever seen clog dancing at. Cheers.

The Good, the Evil and the Pilgrim Poets

In early 1989, in a little office almost directly above the Railway pub on Tithebarn Street, the brother and sister team of Andrew and Lorraine Bowers had just used some of their Enterprise Allowance money to set

themselves up as In-House Productions, a hopeful entertainments pro-
motion company. Andy was a guitarist-singer-songwriter and some-
time-poet with a strong Waterboys influence and also a lot of originality
and energy. His previous band, Came Under Mayne, had recently broken
up, and a main part of the current idea was to launch his own solo
musical career.

The first regular venue chosen for this was the upstairs bar of the Pil-
grim pub on Pilgrim Street, a long thin olde-worlde style room above the
main basement bar. The first couple of events in March and April 1989
were uncertain in style, headlined respectively by the poet Gladys Mary
Coles and by the sculptor Arthur Dooley (reading his favourite bits of
this and that). After this, the event settled quickly into a monthly open-
floor night, emceed by Joe Riley of the *Liverpool Echo*, and with a solid
hardcore of poets and musicians who would also perform each Saturday
afternoon at the Cavern on Mathew Street.

The Pilgrim and Third Room poetry events fertilised and fed each
other, and meanwhile David Symonds had begun a new series of music
nights also open to performance poetry in the Third Room. The live
poetry scene in Liverpool had faltered badly in early 1988, but by two
years later it was the healthiest it had been since the 1960s. Part of this
was undoubtedly due to In-House's conscious attempt to gather a core
of performers to appear together in professional bookings in pubs, clubs
and theatres as well as the regular Pilgrim nights. By the time of Febru-
ary 1990's three-night stint at the Playhouse, this was pretty much
sorted. Singers included Andrew Bowers and Ebony. Comedians
included Mark Bone, the Darwin Brothers and most notably Terry
Kilkelly, who was just perfecting his stage persona and delicately incom-
petent magicianship as Terry Titter. Poets included Terry Caffrey, Dennis
Fontenot and myself. Michael Cunningham was developing his perfor-
mance at this time (as well as his spectacular T-shirt collection); and
with Marian Wilson he formed the duo M & Mz. One of the most
talented poets to emerge in 1989–90 was Kevin Killeen. Originally from
London, he possessed an apparently effortless lyricism that was as
effective on the page as the stage: a sort of modern-day free-verse Dylan
Thomas but without the self-loathing.

Known, for want of a better name, as the Pilgrim Poets, this was the
group that survived the departure of In-House Productions after the
1990 Edinburgh Festival. For the autumn of that year, Ian Alty and
Steve Russell took a confused semblance of control; and in January
1991 Michael Cunningham took over as organiser and main emcee, the

group incidentally benefiting from some crossover from a comedy night at the same venue. New poets in the 1991 Edinburgh Festival team included Eugene Lange and Lizzy London (the recently acquired stage-name of Di Williams, an open-floor regular since mid-1990); and other new Pilgrim regulars included Mandy Coe and Colin Watts. I'd first met Mandy in May at an appalling business skills course we'd both hoped might help us to become self-employed; in the shared conditions of suffering caused by crassly bigoted ex-businessmen posing as lecturers, we'd recognised each other as kindred spirits immediately. Performing her poetry, Mandy had a natural knack for relating to audiences, and quickly became an important member of the group. Surprisingly, considering his drama background, Colin Watts was slower to find his proper voice; but probably it was his awareness of exactly these difficulties that would later help him to coach other poets in finding their own ways of doing it live.

In September 1991, the group got a proper name at last: the Evil Dead Poets Society (for which I take full credit, though Michael Cunningham encouraged me). Carole Baldock – who in 1998 would become coordinator for the group – had appeared on the scene by this time, reading her semi-rhyming poems under the unlikely stage-name of Châ, but pronouncing it 'Tia', as in Tia Maria. No one understood or remembered, and eventually she went for the sensible option and dropped it altogether. Essex-born Matt Wade first performed at the Pilgrim in December, at the Police Helicopter Poetry Competition Performance session. (Incidentally, Mandy Coe won first prize; Dave Evans came second.) A striking new poet was Sarah Cowie. Welsh-American and originally from Baltimore, Sarah Cowie brought a challenging politico-sensual form of poetry you've never heard before, a sense of danger alongside her constant flirting with the audience.

In June 1992 the group held its first one-off guest night, The Evil Dead Poets' Big Night Out, promoted as 'An evening of comedy, poetry, and crass bad taste, with Mark Bone, Matty Thompson, Eugene Lange, David Bateman, Bish and others, almost live...' These nights, initially a tie-in with the Liverpool Festival of Comedy, would run annually for five years until being replaced in 1997 by a Halloween comedy-poetry night.

From July 1992, Kevin McCann and Barbara Murray joined Michael Cunningham in the organising, and with Regional Arts Board project funding set up a series of monthly guest nights to run alongside the monthly open-floor nights, a practice that has been retained into 2001. Of the two group planning meetings that summer, one of them seemed to be mostly taken up by arguments about the group's name: some of the group, including Kevin and Barbara, felt that being an Evil Dead Poets Society could well discourage potential funders and guest poets. Knowing when I was losing an argument, I conceded that the guest nights might have a new name, and reluctantly suggested an idea that I'd never much liked, but that I'd held back for use in an emergency: the Dead Good Poets Society.

Funding came, and in October the first grant-funded guest night featured Michael Donaghy. But things never run quite smoothly: right after that, the EDPS-cum-DGPS lost the Pilgrim to the long-threatened refurbishments and change-of-management, and consequently changed venue to upstairs at the Philharmonic pub for most of 1993. Despite an uneasy relationship with the management, in was in these plush surroundings that the Evil Dead/Dead Good Poets Society took off in a big way, consistently enjoying a surfeit of open-floor poets, and filling the room with audience on the guest nights. Guests from around Britain included Geraldine Monk, Ian McMillan and Poets of the Machine, with many more local guests and support poets. However, the good attendances didn't prevent Phil, the stand-in manager, from summarily ending the arrangement in November. (Refurbishments duly followed.)

The shift across the road to the Flying Picket in the Merseyside Trade Union, Community and Unemployed Resource Centre was made in desperation, but it came as a blessing in disguise; there was the Tolpuddle Bar for open-floor nights and the Flying Picket Theatre for larger guest nights; and it provided a stable venue for two years. Michael Cunningham had dropped out from the organising by now, followed by Kevin McCann's departure from the group in 1994, leaving Barbara Murray as the key organiser with individual events being organised by various members. Barbara Murray was long the sole emcee for the poetry nights: the later rotation of roles began pretty much by chance one night in autumn 1994 when Barbara happened to be late and Brian Stanley Jones ended up emceeing.

In 1994–95, events proliferated. These included exchange gigs. Live poetry organisations in other cities would send teams of poets to perform at the DGPS in Liverpool, and in turn those organisations would host performances by teams of DGPS poets: London, Manchester, Huddersfield, Bradford and Edinburgh were the first five cities. The DGPS also sent teams to compete in 'slams' – live poetry competitions – in various cities, and Glyn Wright was a joint-winner of the 1994 UK National Slam; other wins included the Bristol–Liverpool Inter-City Slam 1995, in which the DGPS won both categories, the Team Prize (David Bateman, Graham Casey, Sarah Cowie and Cynthia Hamilton) and Individual Prize (Cynthia Hamilton). That said, many of the DGPS weren't especially keen on the idea of art as competition, so the DGPS never hosted any slams at this time. As far as I know, the entire Liverpool slam scene consisted of the series of open slams hosted by Ayo at the Largo Bistro in late 1995 to early 1996. From spring 2000, the DGPS cast aside its misgivings about competitive arts for a year, and dabbled with a series of single-round slams: Martin Stannage, Jo Warburton and Alison Rostron were among the winners. (Across the water, the Wirral Ode Show Poets have run an annual open slam in Birkenhead on or around each National Poetry Day since 1998.)

DGPS poets also found themselves doing more local guest appearances from this period, for example on local radio and in a tour of Merseyside libraries. Another significant development was the running of workshops specifically aimed at improving poetry performance. Eugene Lange and I had run one back in August 1992, but from July 1994 onwards workshops became more frequent. Glyn Wright and I ran a series of workshops in early 1995, and more importantly, Colin Watts began teaching a regular evening class for the University of Liverpool – possibly the first accredited course in poetry performance in the UK – which has certainly contributed to the quality of open-floor (and professional) performances in Liverpool over recent years.

Matt Wade and Dave Smith were both prominent open-floor poets at this time, famous as much for their humour as their poetry. As a poet, Dave Smith was no craftsman (for which you can partly blame me, as I was his creative writing tutor), but his floor-spot was almost always one of the high points of the evening. Only one step this side of bonkers, Dave's performance (sometimes with beautiful assistant Pippa) was endearingly eccentric and often hilarious. Miles Hadfield, more crafted, would deliver his near-surreal poems in an even tone of such utter scorn that you were never completely sure how much was wit and how much was bitterness. Another major poet, clearly serious, was Jean Sprackland, who despite having been writing poetry for only two years sprang on to the scene fully formed in early 1994. Restrainedly intense in performance, and seeing herself mostly as a writer for the page, she almost by chance happened to write poems beginning with instant hooks, like 'Love' ('He thinks of it more or less/ as the rest of us think of dog shit') and 'Monopoly' ('He was the sort of man/ who beats his kids/ at Monopoly,/ night after night.').

Eugene Lange dropped out from the group around the end of 1994, and started spreading the first of a series of wild allegations of racism about various Liverpool poets. Though by 1999 his accusations had become more obviously false and abusive, his earlier credibility meant that he almost undoubtedly did some damage to the DGPS (and possibly other local poetry groups) around this time. Eugene is a genuinely talented performer, and it's a shame that there's been no reconciliation.

On 26 July 1995, DGPS hosted a combined guest and open-poetry session in the garden of the Bluecoat Arts Centre. Paul Cosgrove was one of the two dozen advertised poets; never exactly a regular, but always up for a special event, Paul also booked Dead Good Poets for gigs in the wilds of Kirkby, and in April 1998 he was a key person in setting up the Centre for Words at Kirkby Unemployed Centre, running workshops and exchanges, and hosting regular live poetry sessions from autumn 2000 onwards. Dave Smith was another participant in the Bluecoat event: he took part in this and the poetry night at Kelechi's on 27 July, then died in his sleep. Three months later, on 20 October, Lizzy London also died. Autumn 1995 came with crap over everything.

The DGPS was also on the move again, due to major rebuilding work at the Flying Picket (renamed the Picket by this time, in keeping with New Labour moderation). The very last Evil Dead Poets Society open floor at the Picket shared a room with the Levellers Folk Club in October, then in November the open floors shifted to the Largo Bistro on the corner of Seel Street and Colquitt Street. The problem was that at the one-roomed Largo, you couldn't charge on the door, so (though we did have Jean Binta Breeze one night at the Largo) the regular guest nights were held at the Everyman Bistro's Third Room even though it was unavailable on Thursdays, the preferred day of the week. The other problem was that if you keep changing your day of the week, your regulars suddenly stop being regulars. So, desperately sticking to Thursdays, the open floors carried on at the Largo Bistro until the staff there made the decision for us in May 1996 by double-booking us with a disco.

On the brighter side, DGPS found itself hosting a number of book launch performances, several from long-standing local open-floor poets. I think that many of us had had experience of appallingly dry launch events, and it quickly became the intention to make genuine performance nights of these. Also, on the organisational side, April 1996 saw the DGPS move from its previous sequence of one-off project grants to more secure annual funding, allowing more flexibility in planning events. Unfortunately it also meant that I would have less and less excuse to carry on referring to the open-floor nights as the Evil Dead

Poets Society. Becoming a minority of roughly one, even I would abandon the practice by October 1997. But still, for me, there will always be a part of the Dead Good Poets Society that is forever Evil.

Other Sessions, 1995–2001

Through the mid-1990s other sessions came and went. I never made it along to the Kitchen Club, but my spies in spring 1995 reported it as mostly a students' poetry night at the Largo Bistro and notable for its generous quantities of angst. I could be wrong. The spring and summer of 1995 contained some memorably sweaty nights of poetry and drumming upstairs at Kelechi's on Maryland Street, where Nigerian-born poet Esiaba Irobi would manage to cram 40 or 50 people into a bar about the same size as your living room.

More long-lived was 'Free Your Mind', founded in March 1995 by Martin van Teeseling, outspokenly bisexual sculptor-poet. FYM began by running monthly low-key open-floor poetry and music evenings in Toxteth Library on Windsor Street, also the home of the Writing Liaison Office, a key supporter of FYM. Its other main support came from Catalyst Dance and Drama Group, through which FYM came to set up its first one-off performance event as part of the South Liverpool Arts Festival. From August 1995, FYM ran its main open-floor performance nights at the Irish Centre on Mount Pleasant, with proper amplification and where Guinness featured rather more prominently than the orange juice which was the hardest liquor available at Toxteth Library. These sessions would last through to December 1996, after which Martin went to Scotland to become a Buddhist monk. As a surprising twist, Free Your Mind was reformed briefly in April 2000 by Matt Wade, ex of the DGPS and Blue Silver Theatre Company.

In mid-1996 two creative writing undergraduates, Joanne Derbyshire and Barbara Shackley, set up the monthly 'Shenanigans' poetry and music sessions which ran until August 1997. These were at the Largo Bistro, except for three months in late summer 1996 when they performed from a booth to a mostly inattentive audience at Scruffy Murphy's on Hanover Street. Poets John McKeown, Aaron Murdoch and Beryl Phillips all featured there. At this stage there seemed to be an awful lot of organisers, and a lot of arguments and rumour-mongering, but I trust it got better later.

In September 1995 Martin Daws came to Liverpool, and in early 1996 the first 'Poets Get Paid' events occurred: 'a monthly poetry jam. It began as a poem and now it's a club.' Actually, Poets Get Paid was never a regular open-floor session, but rather formed poetry's overlap with the club scene at venues like the Nation, providing a platform for mostly black poets with an emphasis on rap and soul-based poetry. Curtis Watt did some impressive PGP gigs, and the tantalisingly short-lived Imaginary Selves also featured. The later events became fewer and further between, ending around early 1998. However, Martin Daws himself stayed active, and he ran a couple of sessions in Lark Lane in south Liverpool that summer, in the backyard of a cafe-bar that was so ill-equipped it barely existed. It did have a fridge, though. Louise McKenny Wallwein and Jerome Massett both guested in the yard there among the open-floorers.

The little Hub Cafe on Berry Street had been used as a one-off venue several times in 1997 by poets including Mandy Coe, Martin Daws and Colin Watts; and for a while in autumn 1998 there was poetry there every Tuesday night. Separated from the adjacent bicycle shop by only a wire-mesh partition, the Hub boasts furniture made from bicycle parts, so the chairs are better for looking at than sitting on. Here, Elaina ran the fort-nightly 'Pure Poetry' sessions, alternating with Tom George (Mayblin) who'd run his 'Ruby Tuesday' sessions there from about May onwards. Eventually these nights fell victim to the getting-double-booked-with-a-disco syndrome, which is how come Tom George's December 1998 session started in the Hub but actually took place in the Cafe Tabac just round the corner at the top of Bold Street. In the new year, Tom's sessions shifted down the hill to the Acorn Gallery and Egg Cafe in New-ington, and Ruby Tuesday became RubyActive, running a monthly Thursday night session which was still going strong in October 2001.

The Egg, with lots of roof timbers and candles in evidence, was the same loft-like venue used by the Third Room Poets for their final two gigs back in December 1990. Tom George had first thought of it as a likely venue because, since early 1998, he'd been attending Monday night poetry sessions there run by John Bleasdale. John Bleasdale was a lecturer at the University of Liverpool, and the sessions attracted students from both of the central universities. Two regular poets were Ben-nett Huffman and Ralph Pite, with whom John Bleasdale published a joint collection *Tricycle* (1998). After one of the gig posters featured a poetry superhero, the sessions gained the unofficial title of 'Poetry-Boy'; and when John Bleasdale quit, Gaz carried them on. Most recently, the baton was picked up in May 2000 by the grey activist poetry duo Still Life, namely DGPS veterans Beryl Phillips and Pat Fearon, along with satirical singer-guitarist Graham Holland, writer of such classics as

'Never Trust A Panda'. The sessions are now called 'Strut Your Stuff'. One of the things that's made the Egg a good poetry venue is the active interest of various staff. Ben Chesterton, a poet himself, set up several guest poetry nights at the Egg in the past, and often takes part in the open floors there.

It was also at the Egg in early 1998 that Tom George first met Liam Brayd (poetic name of Nick Brady, also known as artist Ernest Klasp), and both would also become regulars at the DGPS events and other open-floor sessions. In March 1999 Liam Brayd, under the working title of Cardboard Underground, began the monthly 'Little Bohemia' sessions upstairs at the Pilgrim, combining poetry and music with occasional comedy. Sound familiar? Liam Brayd had a hankering to be the Brian Epstein of poetry, and was always telling everybody how new and innovative Little Bohemia was, but in fact it was simply a perfectly good open-floor night. All the usual suspects would turn up on occasion, and I once even saw Jalal Nuriddin of the Last Poets perform there. I think that was on the very last night, which was in December 1999.

'Speakers' Corner' was a series of sessions run by Shadrack (previously Shadrock, alias Shane Bennett), who I'd first bumped into at a DGPS night and one of Martin Daws's Lark Lane sessions in 1998. The sessions began in February 1999 at Montanas Wine Bar on Leece Street, just uphill from the bombed-out St Luke's Church; in March it shifted downhill to the Life Cafe Voodoo Room at the bottom of Bold Street, before doing a sharp left to the Zanzibar on Seel Street for July to November. The Anti-Boredom Alliance (i.e. Shadrack) promised a night of poetry, music and comedy 'far better than a kick up the bum (unless you're a masochist)'. Shadrack himself is always a larger-than-life character whenever he goes into deejay-emcee-poet mode, and Speakers' Corner aimed for a club feel, combining the open-floor poetry with music and rapping. IOC performed there, complete with human beatbox, and there'd be some nicely improvised rapping along with the set pieces. With mirrorball and disco lights, being on the stage at the Zanzibar could seem like being in the yard at Colditz: if you were reading your poems from the page you'd better have a good short-term memory to keep the words going in the space until the searchlight comes back.

In April 2000 Skoolofish began their weekly Saturday night Fish 'n' Chips sessions at Montanas (now Hannah's) on Leece Street. Martin Daws and the Transmission MCs, IOC and Tom George were among the various poets and rap crews to speak over the funk and hip hop that spring and summer.

Explosive Mouth was a theatre company founded in 1995 by Kieron Deveney, originally for staging his own plays, and later for presenting work by numbers of people. This included combinations of drama, music and poetry, such as a June 1996 show at the Unity Theatre in collaboration with Joanne Derbyshire and Barbara Shackley (in the process of forming Shenanigans) and featuring poets John McKeown, Aaron Murdoch and Beryl Phillips. The Explosive Mouth open-floor nights began in October 1998 at Brian's Diner on Stanley Street, then ran from January 1999 at Ropes bar on Bold Street. As well as the musicians and some fairly ghastly comedy, regular poets included Baz, Liam Brayd, Tom George, Paul Newton, and a number of the other usual suspects of that time. Explosive Mouth lost its venue at the end of the year, but moved in 2000 to the Hub, staying until the Hub's closure in September, when it shifted to the Picket on Hardman Street, holding its open floors there on the second and fourth Wednesdays of each month.

Skipping briefly across the water to Birkenhead, the 'Wirral Ode Show' deserves a mention. It was long organised by Hazel Eaton and as far as I know, it's the only long-lived series of open-floor poetry sessions to exist in the Wirral since Jabberwocky. Its original inspiration was the result of a brief-lived dodgy venture called 'Poetic Licence' run by John Myers, who around the beginning of 1995 had placed an advert in the *Wirral Globe* saying 'Local literary agent seeks poets.' A few dozen hopeful poets, Hazel among them, turned up at the venue in Birkenhead, where they read out their poetry and were asked to return the following week. By the third 'audition', to which only six poets turned up, it was clear that Myers had no real plan; he'd presumably been hoping some unknown ace performance poets would turn up, so he could cash in on the new rock'n'roll. The half-dozen poets talked among themselves, and Anthony Zausmer suggested to Hazel Eaton and the others that they set up their own poetry sessions, and they agreed.

They held some workshop sessions, the size of the group crept up to about eight people (Carole Baldock was one of the newcomers), and they did a few performances as the Wirral Ode Show. A falling out between Anthony Zausmer and Hazel Eaton meant that nothing happened for a while. Then in autumn 1996, Hazel Eaton and Carol Jackson set up an open-floor night at Birkenhead Cricket Club. These nights were originally quarterly, and there was one more event at the BCC before spells at Lola's 2 in Market Street, and at the Piazza and the Letters pub, both on Argyle Street just off Hamilton Square. Attendances weren't always high, so sometimes they'd simply hold workshops instead of performance nights; but they gradually built up a solid core of poets and audience. Carol Jackson dropped out, but poet Barbara Laing and comedian-poet Graeme Kenna came in on the organising. Other regular poets included Jan McGrann, Phil Martin-Hall and Simon Palin. In 1998, the open-floor nights became monthly, and settled in the basement bar of the Letters pub, remaining there until mid-2000 when, with comic poet Jason Richardson as a new organiser, they shifted venue to Seamus O'Donnell's on Exmouth Street, where they have been running on the last Thursday of each month since.

The Company of Poets

The DGPS open floor had no fixed home in the middle of 1996. After a couple of months in the Everyman Foyer Bar and a spell at the Irish Centre, the DGPS at last gave way to destiny in October, and shifted all its regular events to Wednesdays at the Everyman Bistro's Third Room. It was a spartan sort of room, but it was pretty in pink and yellow, and personally I'd always rated it as a poetry venue. It felt comfortably full with only 30 people, but you always knew you could squeeze 100 in when you needed to. Particularly big hits at the guest nights were Patience Agbabi and Rosie Lugosi, who've returned again and again. Patience Agbabi first appeared with the four-poet group Atomic Lip, and it was this multi-voiced presentation of poetry that inspired the 1997 formation of Flying Fishes–Performance Poets, a six-person team of DGPS regulars Bateman, Coe, Cowie, B. S. Jones (token Scouser), Sprackland and Watts; in 1999, Pat Fearon and Beryl Phillips would form the performance duo Still Life.

Other guests in 1996–97 included Kit Wright, Jackie Kay, Cheryl Martin, Brendan Cleary, Julia Darling and local guests Levi Tafari, Dinesh Allirajah and Glyn Wright (who'd moved on from the open-floor scene after 1995). Away gigs, exchange gigs and workshops continued on an occasional basis; the workshop sessions with musicians were especially fruitful for some poets, and led to a gig in December 1996 featuring Mandy Coe, Sarah Cowie and Barbara Murray performing their poetry with live music.

In 1997 there was sometimes a problem with low attendance at guest nights (and it was no longer possible to blame it on clashes with Euro '96 matches), and this led to the incorporation of a half-hour open floor at those too from the start of 1998, so the DGPS were running two open-floor sessions each month.

Over the years, many of the DGPS open-floor poets had found them-
selves also being booked as support poets – or, more rarely, as main acts
– for DGPS guest poetry nights. But the jump from 5-minute spot to 15-
or 20-minute set could be daunting for inexperienced performers, what-
ever the quality of their poetry, and with this in mind the idea of mini-
support slots was brought in as a gentler transition. The DGPS also
began to develop its links with other regional organisations: these
included collaborative events with Liverpool City Council, Windows
Poetry Project, the Bluecoat Arts Centre and the Wirral Ode Show,
whose poets were featured twice in 1998.

Several of the DGPS's voluntary organisers had long nursed a desire to
make a recording of the poets. In April 1998 Steve Garnett videoed per-
formances by 14 of the poets at Keylink Studios in Kirkby. Launched in
July at the Workhaus Gallery and thereafter marketed with comic incom-
petence, over half of the 21 performances on *The Dead Good Poetry Video* are
quite strikingly impressive. Dinesh Allirajah's acerbic poem 'Mimic'
stands out, as does Sarah Cowie's sultry performance of 'Moon Man':
'Surprising to find your skin prevents/ my hand from reaching further
into you.' Minnie Stacey's 'Me And Time' dips into office fantasies, and
also captures some of the occasionally bizarre skippy-dancey elements of
her performance style. More conventionally, at the open floors and at
restaurant bookings, she'd sing with the poet-singer-guitarist Graham
Casey. Another poet from that time featured on the video was young
Glaswegian Gavin Gibson. Always very sharp and witty, he somehow
managed to combine his deadpan delivery with an enormous friendly
grin. His 'Ode to my Girlfriend', in which he finds his affections torn
between his girlfriend and his other obsession, is a sort of Glaswegian
football equivalent of Sid Hoddes's 'Mashed Potato/Love Poem'.

Quite a few new poets arrived on the scene around May 1998, includ-
ing Liam Brayd, who'd been writing for some years. In a ham-melodra-
matic voice he'd orate from his series of first-person free-verse accounts
of his many alternative dream-lives, sometimes a bit comic, sometimes
a bit poignant, and always very surreal, very strange. A quality item.
Tom George, a student who'd arrived from Sheffield at the end of 1997,
wrote a mixture of whimsies, celebrations of the little pleasures of life,
love poetry, and little comments on society, often consciously using the
rhythms of pop. Barry Bristow, always known as plain Baz, was often an
extraordinary performer. There was no particular boundary between his
poetry and his songs, and he'd sing or speak in his distinctive voice,
resulting from a partial cleft palate. Sometimes he'd use his little key-

board; sometimes he'd dance his poems to recordings he'd made earlier. It didn't always quite work, but it often did, and he had a couple of absolutely classic audience-participation poems, 'Ah, That's Better!' and 'The Wild Turquoise Underpants'. Derek Jones, master of the forced stress, would give wonderfully flawed performances: exuberantly declaimed by heart, with an almost guaranteed brief failure of memory in at least one poem. My own favourite from Degsy is the emphatic minimalist poem 'Too Much Too Quick Too Soon'. Another new figure was Jim Bennett, a veteran of the 1960s live poetry scene who'd been going to O'Connor's back in the days when he was too young to. Beat-influenced and very prolific, he was also doing readings in the USA under the cryptically crude pseudonym of Richard Dripping. He also wrote and sang songs and played guitar, but was mostly too shy about it for his own good. In August 2000 Long Neck Media released Jim Bennett's CD *Down In Liverpool*. At times reminiscent of Adrian Henri and Andy Roberts, it's a nice bunch of poems and songs.

Behind the scenes, the organisation of the DGPS was going through what's probably best described as a long slow crisis. Becoming an annually funded organisation in spring 1996 had created a greater pressure for accountability and clear rules in the organisation as a whole, which by itself wasn't a problem. However, the organisation had become so dependent on Barbara Murray that when Barbara withdrew from her central role in June 1997, it soon became clear that, with all the DGPS's activities, no one person had a clear idea or firm hold of everything that was going on. (I should mention that I was the nominal chair from this time, so none of this says much for my own organisational skills.) Barbara tried to ease the transition, but the work seemed to have multiplied, partly because more activities meant more work, but also because the lack of a central coordinating figure made everything that much more messy. It had all got a lot more complicated than the days when it was just a case of booking a bar-room once a month and putting out a few posters and leaflets. In September 1998 the DGPS and North West Arts Board agreed that DGPS would have an official coordinator – paid, as it turned out, for a bare four hours per week – and Carole Baldock was elected to the post in December.

Yet in fact things would get worse, and then only very gradually get better. Sarah Cowie had long been central to the group, and Gordon Dunne was the book-keeper; in September 1998, Sarah left Liverpool, soon to return to Baltimore, and in December, Gordon died. Feelings aside, this meant that things were briefly even more shambolic than before.

There comes a time in the life of a growing organisation when it has to face up to the fact that though it may still perceive itself as young and struggling, it's actually achieved a degree of success, and that younger and more struggling organisations perceive it as old and privileged, and want the things it's got. From the latter part of 1998, there was new blood in the DGPS planning group, which should have improved its wobbly state. However, the new blood included the organisers of the other local poetry groups, who naturally had their own agendas, as well as that of the DGPS, at heart. So DGPS planning meetings, already busy and frustrating just because of the business of sorting out future guest nights, exchanges, workshops, away gigs and general practical bits and pieces, now became bogged down in the business of other groups and their relationships to the DGPS. For a while, this essentially came down to other groups trying to use DGPS money rather than finding their own elsewhere, while simultaneously not actually contributing much in the way of work towards DGPS events.

Volunteers' precious time began to seem wasted, as more and more meeting time was taken up with lengthy speeches about how new and dynamic and innovative Cardboard Underground was, and how correspondingly old and static and staid was DGPS. Even simple items of business were made almost impossible to get through. Decisions that had already been agreed were now argued over and over. In one sad instance of bureaucracy-as-an-end-in-itself, someone demanded that compulsory monthly meetings be written into the constitution, then also demanded that the volunteer book-keeper bring copies of the accounts for everyone at every meeting. With this constant bickering and confrontational atmosphere, even people with good intentions were likely to be suspected of harbouring hidden motives. After a few months of this sort of thing, members of the various poetry groups were at each other's throats; and because most people were participants in most groups, there was a complex pattern of shifting loyalties.

The Liverpool Poetry Festival in October 1999 brought this all wonderfully to a head. Originally Liam Brayd's idea and discussed at DGPS meetings, this was intended as a cooperative venture between the DGPS, Cardboard Underground, Explosive Mouth and RubyActive. It consisted of a series of open-floor sessions (three by Cardboard Underground, one by DGPS) with mini-guest spots funded by DGPS, one local guest session organised by Explosive Mouth, a guest night headlined by Lemn Sissay at the Bluecoat (organised by DGPS), and a Friday night gig at the Picket Theatre headlined by Chloë Poems – gay socialist transvestite, gingham diva and effeminate son and daughter of Scotland Road – supported by various mini-guests (a combined DGPS–Cardboard Underground session).

Problems emerged early on: DGPS had originally booked John Cooper Clarke, who turned out to have been double-booked. Then a series of posters and leaflets appeared with key DGPS information missing and claiming that the whole festival was organised by Cardboard Underground. Then Cardboard Underground mysteriously forgot to get in touch with the DGPS co-organiser, Degsy Jones, who was arranging the booking of Chloë Poems. The Chloë Poems night became the most controversial, with Stuart Todd, Baz and a couple of others managing to be outraged that such outrageous poetry should come to Liverpool to outrage them.

At the end-of-festival gathering at the Pilgrim, where Kieron Deveney was at pains to publicly emphasise that the DGPS had played no part whatsoever in organising the festival, Liam, Kieron and Baz announced the formation of the Liverpool Association of Musicians, Poets and Performers, a forum for discussion of how live poetry and so on could work better in Liverpool. Suspecting LAMPP to be another instrument for the purposes of Cardboard Underground rather than those of performers in general, many couldn't be bothered with it, and after about three meetings it quietly vanished. Gradually, most people collected their deposits back from the High Horse Hire Company, and got back down to the ordinary practical business of live poetry in Liverpool. Liam and Baz gave up poetry at the end of 1999, telling DGPS it was all their fault. (Not quite: Baz was thoroughly disillusioned with LAMPP as well.) Liam told a DGPS meeting how disappointed he was with everybody, and that he wasn't coming any more.

The year 2000 saw the DGPS, RubyActive, Explosive Mouth and Strut Your Stuff continue their regular open floors, and the DGPS combined open-floor-cum-guest nights have already featured many poets from Liverpool and farther afield, including Chloë Poems, Brian Wake, Tony Dash, Rosie Lugosi, David Bateman, Paul Lyalls, Sue Dymoke and James Quinn. Roger McGough made a surprise appearance as an open-floor poet, and Alison Rostron, a regular open-floorer over the previous year, gave a very effective performance in her first guest appearance in April. This is the business.

The year 2000 also saw the emergence of Club Surreal as a regular open floor in Liverpool. The brainchild of compère-comedian Gonzo (alias Hans Schmidt) and woodwind-player Geni, Club Surreal had previously existed in Germany, London and Oxford before arriving at the

Brewery on Berry Street. Mostly known for the quality of the jazz, the Sunday events also feature open-floor poets and comedians, as well as regular musicians jamming with the guests.

In March 2001 a United Nations poetry performance at the Unity Theatre shared the bill with the DGPS's first South Asian Arts Show-case, a show fusing poetry, music and dance. In April, the Dead Good Poets Society shifted venue back to its first home, the upstairs bar at the Pilgrim. And it's worth mentioning that despite all the fraughtness surrounding the planning of the Liverpool Poetry Festival back in October 1999, similar festivals followed in 2000 and 2001, and it's nice to see that the various poetry groups can at least sometimes manage to coordinate with each other.

Slim Volumes and Fat Ones

In opening this essay, I mentioned the separation between regular poetry nights and the literary establishment; back when I first went to By Word Of Mouth, I don't think there was a single person there who had a 'proper' book out. On the other hand there were the small presses, including local ones. The latter included Sylvia Hikins's Toulouse Press, and the publishing arm of the Windows Poetry Project run by Dave Ward and Dave Calder, and these produced both magazines and book-lets as a further platform for the more publishable of the live poets. The Hikinses co-authored two collections: *A Black Look on the Bright Side* (1972) and *Harold and Sylvia Hikins's Book of Revelations* (1974, with taste-ful nude photo of authors on back cover); Toulouse also published *Poems About...* by Sid Hoddes (1976), and booklets by Dave Ward and Dave Calder, both of whom went on to find wider publication. Published between 1982 and 1987, the Windows Poetry Minibooks Series of some three dozen A6 16-page booklets included several of the regulars on the live poetry scene.

But magazines and the occasional booklet apart, there was a decided lull through the 1980s into the early 1990s. In 1993, Dave Ward's *Jambo* – a kind of pictorial poetic novel about its eponymous hero, blending gritty dole-queue urban realism with witty logical conceits – was at last published by Impact of London; and closer to home, Other Publications published Kevin McCann's first full-length collection, *Mirror, Mirror,* with its recurring themes of difference, persecution, loss and longing.

1995 saw books from two of the Evil Dead/Dead Good Poets Society's regulars. Michael Cunningham's *Sharp and Leathery* contains some pointed and witty fantasy pieces, as well as his more observational poems; the world of crime is seldom far away, with an incisive overlapping of the languages of business and violence here and there: 'Hard men talk staccato...' In November, Spike published Glyn Wright's first collection, *Could Have Been Funny*, which became a Poetry Book Society Choice as well as being short-listed for the T. S. Eliot Prize and winning the Aldeburgh Poetry Festival Prize. Essentially a series of poetic monologues, the book is peopled with characters ranging from the sympathetic through to the starkly homicidal: soldiers, sailors, suffering wives, steelworkers; everywhere, characters in these poems are facing (or avoiding facing) lives that haven't quite gone as planned.

In 1996 Iron Press of Tyneside published my own *Curse Of The Killer Hedge*. Ian McMillan read it and said, 'David Bateman's poems come directly from the pub, the music-hall, and the street. He's a kind of top-gear Gavin Ewart on the top deck of a local bus.' He didn't actually say he liked it, but I'm always grateful for the quote, not least because it prompted me to read Gavin Ewart, who I'd bizarrely not discovered until then. In 1997 Spike published another prize-winning book, Jean Sprackland's *Tattoos For Mothers Day*. Her poetry, often very sensual, deals with the small magic – light or dark – of everyday life, and frequently with ordinary lives on the edge of disaster, or with lives just beyond it. The unspoken is always important, the situations portrayed often dense with emotion in moments of silence. As Mark Robinson wrote, 'Her poems are warm and tender, but with a chilly edge to them, an unspoken punchline that hits all the harder for its silence.'

In December 2000 Spike also published Mandy Coe's first collection, *Pinning the Tail on the Donkey*, which has received acclaim from such poets as Patience Agbabi, Julia Darling and Fred Voss. More explicitly political than most poets, a gentle streak of self-questioning runs through her work, not just in her idiosyncratic perceptions but also in the full sense of being part of the society whose foibles she documents.

These are individual achievements; but a more representative selection of poetry comes from the small press magazines, booklets and anthologies of the time. Following Edward Lucie-Smith's seminal anthology of 1967, *The Liverpool Scene,* something of the late 1960s and early 1970s scene was captured in *Roll The Union On!* (edited by Sylvia Hikins, 1973) which also remains the closest thing to a general anthology of Liverpool poetry.

In 1992, Headland published *Lightyears,* edited by Anne Cunningham and others. Subtitled *The First Collection of Merseyside Women's Writing,* this is a wide-ranging and patchy book, but very good at its best, and contains quite a few of the poets to be seen performing live in the 1980s and 1990s. R. D. Tameem and Cathy Trimble (abetted by Leroy Cooper) edited the chunky 1990 anthology of south Liverpool poetry, art and photography *Undercurrents,* which includes Dennis Fontenot, Muhammad Khalil/Eugene Lange, Levi Tafari and some two dozen poets, including Jalal Nuriddin and Sulaiman el Hadi of the Last Poets.

In 1993, Carole Baldock published an anthology booklet called *Graffiti: Works of Art as Performed at the Philharmonic Pub,* featuring a dozen DGPS regulars and a couple of guests besides. The reason for the rather coy title is that this was in the middle of the rows about whether the group was called the Evil Dead Poets Society or the Dead Good Poets Society or both. The CD *Poetry Now* (1996, Liverpool Arts and Culture Unit) is the most wide-ranging commercially available audio document of 1990s Liverpool poetry. Disappointingly, a few of the recordings are so muddy as to be almost unlistenable, and the absence of a track listing means you have to guess which poet is which, but there are good performances from Dinesh Allirajah, Terry Caffrey, Sarah Cowie and many others. The 1998 *Dead Good Poetry Video,* though likewise featuring only studio performances, is still probably the best commercially available document of Liverpool's live poetry sessions in the 1990s. Some of the DGPS open-floor sessions through 2000 were recorded, but it remains to be seen whether the material ever gets issued.

Returning to the printed page, in February 2000 the DGPS started publishing its own annual anthology *Brand New Bag,* which aims to include the best of the open-floor poetry; and Headland Publications will be publishing an anthology of the Dead Good Poets Society in early 2002.

Conclusion

Though the poets are all different, there's been a striking continuity in the regular live poetry sessions in Liverpool from the late 1960s through to the new millennium, primarily through the long-lived By Word Of Mouth sessions, and later through the group which began under In-House Productions, known for a while as the Pilgrim Poets, then as the Evil Dead Poets Society, and latterly as the Dead Good Poets Society. The gap between the demise of By Word Of Mouth in May 1988 and the first Pilgrim poetry night in March 1989 was spanned by the Third Room poetry sessions which ran (with breaks) from April 1988 to December 1990, keeping the participants in touch and active in live poetry. Indeed, in a world where poets are generally the most reluctant (and worst) organisers you could imagine, it was probably the experience gained in helping to run the Third Room Poets that enabled Mike Cunningham and Barbara Murray to save the Pilgrim Poets from falling to bits when In-House ceased to exist.

Alongside this succession, other series of sessions have come and gone, usually with a crossover of poets and other performers, often with collaborative events, and occasionally with that cattiness that makes coteries cosier. The Dead Good Poets Society, RubyActive, Explosive Mouth, Strut Your Stuff and Club Surreal are those in existence in October 2001. Probably one or two of these will have stopped by this time next year and probably one or two new ones will have started. Poets and audiences will be performing, listening and of course, drinking. More new bad poets will carry on appearing. And more bad poets will carry on turning into good ones.

Note

It was one night in January 1996 at Peter Kavanagh's pub in Egerton Street, just after an Evil Dead/Dead Good Poets Society planning meeting, that Sarah Cowie first suggested I should write about Liverpool poetry. She actually meant the EDPS-cum-DGPS, but that moment was the beginning of my project on the history of poetry in Liverpool in general, now being researched and written as a book to be published by Headland.

This essay is one area of that project, the area that Sarah was originally thinking of. It's in the nature of the regular live poetic beast that it tends to be only sporadically documented, and that people's memories of it fade, or were never very clear to begin with, owing to the key role of beer and wine in a pursuit that is as hedonistic as it is literary. So in researching this, though I've talked with scores of people, it's inevitable that I've missed out some people and events that ought to have been mentioned; and it's equally inevitable that I've made some mistakes. So I'll say sorry now, and get it over with. But my research on Liverpool poetry (from the seventeenth century right up to the present) is ongoing, so I'll welcome any corrections to errors and any information about Liverpool poetry likely to be useful in the final book. I can be contacted care of Liverpool University Press.

Dead Good Poets, Dead Good Poetry

Carole Baldock

As the man said (gloomily), nobody writes poetry when they're happy. Undeniably, many people take it up as therapy, though a glint of talent enables them to move on to bigger and better things. So I'll own up: despite having had my first piece published at the age of 11 (OK, in the school magazine, a cunning pastiche on Browning's *My Last Duchess*), I turned to poetry with a vengeance after divorcing my husband. The matter was compounded not long after with a big fat dose of unrequited love. Moving swiftly on (a good decade further on), I certainly never pictured myself ending up as coordinator of the Dead Good Poets Society in 1998. Yes, it's a tricky job and somebody's got to do it, though concentrating on administration uses up so much time and energy that it plays havoc with your creative side. But as we all know, it's not just poets who chorus 'Art for Art's sake – money for God's sake.'

Now, it's one thing churning out poems in the privacy of your own home, but quite another jumping in at the deep end, or rather, up onto a stage, and declaiming them in front of a room full of other people. Admittedly, a bare half-dozen in the audience is even more alarming, but all performance poets have been there. Pity it wasn't at the same time, mind you, or it would have amounted to a decent-sized audience. What with location and locals (while playing away as it were) to contend with, and a liberal helping of stage fright, you begin to ask yourself: What on earth do you think you're doing?

My worst moment was a crash course in the classics. In 1992, invited to perform on national AIDS day, the set was to include my own work (mostly humorous) plus a lengthy, elegiac piece, written for the event by a man who'd been diagnosed HIV positive, to be read to the accompaniment of a taped compilation of Elgar's music (I still get shivers whenever I hear it). I'd never done anything like this before. So, two days to rehearse, plus the day job – i.e., intensive research for a dissertation for my degree, then a room full of people (as for press coverage, they took some photos outside, made their excuses and left), and a massive ghetto blaster which kept playing up. But at the end, among all the congratulations, a woman came up and clasped my hands, saying she'd been in tears, laughing and crying. It was all so amazing, particularly in comparison with what seemed like interminable suffering. I decided then and there that I never, ever wanted to feel so wretched again, and other than the occasional pang, performing no longer bothers me.

Just as well, with another treat to come, at one of Liverpool's most famous hotels; naming no names, let's just say the Greeks had a word for it (as do most people who've been there, long before that notorious documentary). Scene of the annual Beatles' Convention, somebody had the bright idea of putting poets on to do readings in between the bands. Somebody should have done a little research first. It was already surreal – for example, four young lads from Argentina who looked just like the Beatles, sang just like them, yet could not otherwise speak a word of English. Four of us were invited along for midday, but started off around 4pm, by which time I had been quenching my thirst, shall we say, but not eating since we were assuming that we'd be going for a meal any minute.

The hotel was packed: fans, bands and stalls and stalls of memorabilia. The room where we would be reading was huge, miles bigger than the smoky, intimate little pubs we usually performed in, with two whopping video screens either side of the stage. Alas, I began to suspect that the first two poets were not going down too well from the reaction of the woman seated nearby, who addressed her mate thus: 'Bloody hell, not more bloody poetry. You comin'? I'm off for a bloody drink.' Nothing to lose, then. Up I went to read two other poets' pieces about the Beatles, and one of my own (when asked if I had anything suitable – swiftly doctoring one about pop culture ('Bolan' being a close rhyme to 'John') – the answer was 'I have now'). Actually, 'read' isn't the right word; I was shouting rather loudly, but it apparently did the trick, catching the audience's attention enough to ensure applause. I came offstage to the strange but sincere compliment: 'You bullied them into that!'

To return to the other kind of reading: with enough poems over the past ten years to fill a drawer, as Peter Finch half-seriously suggests, citing Gillian Clarke, in *The Poetry Business*, my millennium resolution was to put together the classic slim volume. The traditional way has always been to publish widely first, but nowadays, many dive headfirst into publication (and often end up with empty pockets, thanks to vanity publishing). However, it is more sensible to build up an audience first, and since poetry matures with its writer, you may feel, as Liz Lochhead claims on seeing her early work, that you want to buy it all up so that other people can't. For all that poetry is said to be the highest art, writing as a career option is detrimental in that it is the first thing to suffer when making a living, because in itself it rarely pays.

Nonetheless, I firmly believe that being a poet informs your work, enhancing flow, style, metaphor and technique, so all due respect for its role in success. Since I took up a full-time career as a freelance writer in 1993, I've had four books published, and a dozen schools information packs, from literature guides to tomes on bullying, produced by Knight & Bishop. I've also contributed to American journals and the *Children's Britannica*, and written for a wide variety of magazines, including *New International Event* and *The Good Book Guide*.

Going back to my roots and those first scribbled attempts: well, closet poets abound, and when they do venture forth, their next step tends to be joining a writers' group or a workshop. Then, a giant leap: aiming for publication. There still seems to be a huge divide between page and stage, the former accused of elitism, the latter sneered at for poor quality. I came out in the late 1980s after reading in *Poetry Review* a tasty description of the Pilgrim Poets aka the Evil Dead Poets: 'a subtle blend of poetry, music, comedy, herbs and spice (without the herbs and spices)'. Thus spake Michael Cunningham. His life as a performer started when the editor of *Smoke*, Dave Ward, who held a monthly surgery in Walton library, suggested he went to Harold Hikins's reading group, 'By Word Of Mouth', at the Flying Picket. There he met other local poets: David Bateman, Glyn Wright, Dave Symonds, Colin Watts, Eugene Lange (Muhammad Khalil), Levi Tafari, Mandy Coe, Barbara Murray and Rona Campbell. However, this group was to disband when Rona set up the Third Room poets at the Everyman Bistro. After that came the Pilgrim Poets, courtesy of Andrew Bowers, poet and singer/ songwriter, together with Joe Riley, arts editor of the *Liverpool Echo*.

Venues, it's true, have come and gone: the Philharmonic (pub, that is); the Picket; the Largo. For a few years we went back the Third Room, then the Pilgrim pub once more. Poets, too, are moving up and moving on – some, sadly, gone for good: popular, talented writers like Lizzie London, Dave Smith and Gordon Dunne. However, it was in the Pilgrim that the group officially was born, thanks to Sarah Cowie (a multitalented performer, now returned to the US) and Kevin McCann, with many sessions devoted to choosing a suitable nomenclature. And over the years, we have indeed welcomed many dead good poets: Joolz, Cheryl Martin, SuAndi, Michael Donaghy, Simon Armitage, Henry Normal. One of our great strengths is the range of talent displayed on the open floor, poems on every theme you could think of (and some that wouldn't cross your mind in a million years); it's a community effort, from students to OAPs and from novices to writers published in their own right, many of them involved in related activities like workshops.

And while the rest of you were busy celebrating the millennium, we had our 11th anniversary. Several other groups have sprung up, including RubyActive, Explosive Mouth and Cardboard Underground; also new in town was the first Liverpool Poetry Festival. This was a week-long event of poetry, music, singing and comedy from local performers, and featured Lemn Sissay on National Poetry Day in conjunction with Bluecoat Chambers, with Chloë Poems the following night. Once funding is in place, this may be run annually.

Our events receive considerable support from local media, especially Radio Merseyside, which publicises the DGPS programme and further promotes it by arranging readings with our guest poets. A broadcast of *Write Now* in 2000 featured Derek Jones, David Bateman and Still Life (Pat Fearon and Beryl Phillips, who also perform independently). Experiments included 'Poets Get Paid' and 'Open Invitation', which encouraged performers old and new while the audience voted for the best set by putting their money where their mouth is (well, 50p, anyway). The winner received half the pot, and the chance of performing as support at a future guest evening. We also plan to visit new venues in the city with 'Out in the Open...', aiming eventually to infiltrate the entire Northwest region.

Our mailing list is constantly expanding as we improve contacts with local organisations of all kinds, although predominantly in the arts. This does not only happen locally; October 1999 saw the launch of the Liverpool issue of *Ambit*, featuring regulars from the DGPS including Colin Watts, David Bateman, Mandy Coe and myself. Many Liverpool organisations now approach us for advice and information, and to arrange performances such as the international Liverpool festival 'WOW: Writing on the Wall'. The publication of a Dead Good anthology should occur in 2002, with a marketing campaign incorporating posters and poetry postcards.

We also intend to continue collaborating with other organisations. Our involvement with the Windows Project's 'Writers on Tour' scheme goes back some years, and two of our most successful evenings included Debjani Chatterjee and Matthew Sweeney. Standing room only is praise in itself, and also shows respect for local support: Mandy Coe and Dinesh Allirajah, and Tom George, who runs his own events, Ruby-Active, at The Egg cafe. Similarly, we hope to be setting up partnerships with theatres such as the Unity, arranging a couple of large-scale events each year featuring the UK's best-known poets. No matter who tops the bill, we can provide first-class support.

Our programme will be expanded even further by organising more exchanges, following successful forays involving Sheffield ('Off the Shelf' festival) and Lincoln, where our visit inspired the hosts to start its own exchange programme starting off with DGPS reading at various venues including the Sun cafe, the Duke of Wellington pub and Ottakars bookshop. In the past, we've visited many different places: the Edinburgh Fringe, Huddersfield, London, Bristol, Cardiff and Birkenhead (home of the Wirral Ode Show, or WOSP set up by Hazel Eaton). A promising start came via a grant of £500 from the Merseyside Special Activities Fund for a visit to Dublin, to strengthen the existing links between the two cities and invite Irish poets, including Maighread Medbh, back to Liverpool.

The Liverpool poets of the 1960s are renowned worldwide, and some may say we have a lot to live up to. However, the Dead Good Poets Society has clearly established that poetry in Liverpool is still alive and kicking.

All You Need is Words

Spencer Leigh

As I'm married to a librarian, all my books are neatly filed. I have a shelf of poetry books and it is a wonderful reminder of the 1960s and early 1970s in Liverpool. Some of the poets had their work published by major publishers or national presses (Adrian Henri and Roger McGough by Jonathan Cape, Brian Patten by Allen and Unwin, Henry Graham by Andre Deutsch, Spike Hawkins by Fulcrum); some by local presses (Brian Jacques, Dave Calder, Sid Hoddes, Matt Simpson, Richard Hill and Malcolm Barnes by Raven Books: Matt, Sid, Nigel Walker and David Porter by Toulouse Press); and some by themselves (Harold and Sylvia Hikins). Then there's the best-selling *Mersey Sound* volume in the Penguin Modern Poets series and Edward Lucie-Smith's *The Liverpool Scene*. I also have copies of the booklets published for the Merseyside festivals of poetry, Brian Patten's magazine *Underdog*, and Russell Pemberton's *Contrasts*. It's a formidable collection – maybe 3,000 poems by local authors – and over the years I have thrown away just as many to make space. Most of all I regret discarding Richard Hill's *Hard Up*, a witty collection heavily inspired by Roger McGough.

McGough, Henri and Patten dominated the early years of the Liverpool scene and created the atmosphere in which poetry performances could flourish. Henri stayed, and their influence can be seen in all the other poets. They themselves were an intriguing mix. Roger McGough with his high-speed delivery had the best puns in Liverpool; Adrian Henri was lyrical and autobiographical and quite open in his desire for A-level schoolgirls; Brian Patten was a traditional romantic with a modern cutting edge. At Merchant Taylors' school in Crosby, I had been taught by 'Yogi' Shepherd that writing lists made bad poetry, but when I started going to readings I discovered that Adrian Henri did it all the time – 'Without You', 'I Want to Paint', 'Me' and 'Tonight at Noon' were all great lists, so Yogi was wrong.

I went to many poetry readings – maybe 100 or more – and I don't think I ever groaned when I saw who was on the bill. Even if derivative, everyone had something to offer and every evening there was something to think about or amuse you. My main gripe was that poets repeated their poems too often; Harold Hikins said that he would read 'Lament for Three Young Men' at every reading until the Vietnam war was over. In contrast, Jim Doran, a *Crosby Herald* reporter, believed that poems, like journalism, were only for the moment. He would read his poems and and tear them up as he went along. His performances ended in a shower of confetti. As I can't remember any of his poems, maybe he was doing the right thing.

I read a few myself, my worst moment coming in O'Connor's Tavern when the sculptor Arthur Dooley interrupted me in a Vietnam poem to ask 'Which fucking side are you on?' Fearing a thump, I said 'If you let me finish, you'll find out' and I spouted some rubbish to make it look as though I couldn't be more anti-American if I tried. My original poem wasn't particularly pro-American, but it served me right for writing about things I didn't understand.

Edward Lucie-Smith's book is dedicated to 'The Beatles without whom &c' and that is the key to the phenomenon. There are so many similarities between the Liverpool poets and the Mersey Beat musicians that they outweigh any differences. Liverpool, as everyone knows and as can easily be proved, is a city of entertainment. Even prior to the 1960s, popular singers (Lita Roza, Frankie Vaughan, Russ Hamilton) and comedians (Tommy Handley, Arthur Askey, Ted Ray, Ken Dodd) came from the city. Everything exploded in the early 1960s with the advent of Mersey Beat, with over 300 groups performing in the city and its suburbs. In order to compete, other forms of entertainment had to be as enticing. The Spinners turned traditional folk music into popular entertainment. One folk duo, Jacqui and Bridie, featured Arthur the Poet and they recorded some of his works. Many country musicians added a beat to their music and for a time, Liverpool was known as the Nashville of England.

Both musicians and poets were heavily influenced by US culture. The genesis of the Liverpool poets lay in San Francisco's Beat scene, and Adrian Henri's style is very close to Allen Ginsberg's. Just as the Mersey musicians covered songs by Chuck Berry and Little Richard, many of the Liverpool poets wrote their own versions of Beat poetry. Significantly, Adrian Henri quoted The Coasters' 'Along Came Jones' in a poem that likened Liverpool to the Wild West. Many of the Liverpool poems refer to US culture and Adrian, Roger and Brian were inspired by the camp *Batman* TV series to write 'Batpoem', 'Goodbat, Nightman' and 'Where Are You Now, Batman?' respectively.

The Beat generation involved poets, artists and musicians and this applied to Liverpool as well. In an attempt to copy the US, a couple of happenings were staged at the Cavern; and then in 1967 we had the real thing when Yoko Ono presented one at the Bluecoat Chambers. Scouse humour was never far away from these events. I recall Yoko Ono being wrapped in bandages and John Gorman of Scaffold shouting out 'You're wanted on the phone.'

The art school was well represented in both music and poetry. It was inevitable as the art school combined a bohemian lifestyle, plenty of free time and the ability to get posters done cheaply. John Lennon, who published his schoolboy poems, is the key example, and there were the painters and lecturers Adrian Henri and Henry Graham. Henry was the grumpiest of the Liverpool poets, the Van Morrison of Liverpool, and he even read a poem chastising the rain because it made him wet!

Music was an integral part of the poetry events. In London the combination was poetry and jazz, but although Adrian Henri named 'Tonight at Noon' after a Charlie Mingus album and Scaffold took their name from a Miles Davis soundtrack, there were few jazz references. Adrian Henri and Roger McGough often worked with the guitarist Andy Roberts, who was studying law at Liverpool University. McGough was part of the poetry and music group Scaffold with Mike McCartney and John Gorman, and they had top ten hits with 'Thank You Very Much' and a modified rugby club song 'Lily the Pink'; Adrian and Andy merged with Mike Evans (Clayton Squares) and Mike Hart (Roadrunners) to form Liverpool Scene, a poetry and rock band which played the Isle of Wight Festival.

Mike Hart was my favourite performer on the poetry circuit. He carried his lyrics in well-worn exercise books and would lay them out in front of him. He rasped his way through very personal songs – 'Almost Liverpool 8', 'Arty's Wife' and, days after a casual relationship with a married woman, 'Nell's Song'. One song began 'Friday got a Ribble bus, Noticed fares had gone up' and I was supremely impressed that someone could write about such a local and everyday way of life. He was an intelligent man – I saw him complete a *Times* crossword in five minutes, though I have no idea if they were the right answers – but he made little money from his music.

He served at a children's clothing stall in the hip Aunt Twacky's Market but he had such bad acne that I wouldn't think any child would go near him. When I foolishly booked him to perform at an open evening at Crosby Civic Hall, I caught him peeing in the new sink in his dressing room – not, of course, that he would be dressing for the stage. He had mental problems and was last heard of in Edinburgh ten years ago. Shame; he could have been Liverpool's answer to Bob Dylan.

Nearly all the poetry events I attended had some acoustic music and sometimes the personal songs outshone the poems. I recall John Cornelius breaking up with his girlfriend Ruth and, like Mike Hart, the bitterness of his feelings was exposed in a remarkably intense performance in a Liverpool pub.

The poetry evenings took place all over Liverpool and, like the Cavern Beat shows, there were usually several performers on one bill. I particularly liked the evenings that Harold Hikins and Sidney Hoddes organised at the Why Not? pub in Harrington Street. Sidney's evenings were more structured than Harold's as Harold, a committed communist, believed that everyone had a right to be heard and so anyone who wanted to read had a platform to do so. Up to 60 or 70 people would crowd into the pub, and sometimes you thought 60 or 70 were going to read their own poems.

Sometimes bigger events were planned. The Valentine's Day Love-In at the Everyman Theatre sounded too good to miss but it promised more than it delivered. The evening started with Mike Hart reciting Chairman Mao's *Little Red Book* to a crashing rock beat and this took up most of the first half. The programme included a letter of support from John Lennon – the letter was 'F'.

Undoubtedly inspired by the 'Wholly Communion' international poetry reading at the Albert Hall in 1965, Harold Hikins and his Merseyside Poetry Committee organised the Big Poetry Night at the Philharmonic Hall on 22 January 1971. It was a unique event: commercially, the 1,800 seats were *philled out* and artistically, it was even more successful. Adrian Henri topped the bill of front-line Liverpool poets and there was music from the Liverpool Fisherman, Highly Inflammable and Foxworthy's Carton. The last-named group included the poet Edwin George, who used to tell audiences that he was going blind.

The Big Poetry Night was followed by a second, which, although very good, was less successful because the novelty had worn off, and the egos had landed meaning that everybody wanting to be included. It was not so much that the poets wanted to perform at the Philharmonic, but that they would feel second rate if they weren't invited. Geoff Speed from Radio Merseyside's *Folk Scene* recorded the second concert but the tapes were not broadcast and although I have them in my possession, I can't play them as I would need a reel-to-reel four-track machine. I do recall Adrian Henri performing his evocative *Autobiography* so superbly to music.

Some of the poets would be ideal guests for the Radio 4 programme *In the Psychiatrist's Chair* as it was so hard to determine what motivated them. Spike Hawkins was the oddest, writing short, manic poems full of absurdities. I open his 1968 collection, *The Lost Fire Brigade*, now and I wonder how I could have paid good money to see him. He was none too keen on getting this good money, incidentally; I once saw him burn his fee as he read a poem. His poems were short and surrealistic and his 'greatest hit' would be 'tree army poem':

> Alert ruin!
> they shout from the trees
> stupid bloody acorns.

No, I've no idea what it means either, but try this:

> The fish counted
> up to 84 and then
> fell off the edge
> of the then known
> world.

Nevertheless, there are about ten Spike Hawkins poems that I know by heart and I can't say that for many poets. Strange days indeed.

The long, straggly Dave Calder looked as though he hadn't had a decent meal in weeks, which he probably hadn't as he was a vegan with little money. Dave was a law graduate from Liverpool University who was sucked into the poetry scene. 'Cube' is the story of his nervous breakdown. Still, he was very lucky with women, who loved his poems about unicorns forgiving them and the like. He was an introverted performer yet there was something magical about him whispering his poems. He influenced many other poets such as Dave Ward, who organised many events and did much to encourage the writing of poetry. Like e. e. cummings and several copycat Liverpool poets (Richard Hill. Edwin George, Spike Hawkins) Dave Calder rarely used capital letters, but this was in keeping with his personality, which was definitely, and probably defiantly, lower case.

Like the beat groups, the Liverpool poets were largely white, male and well-educated. Some were middle-aged. Harold Hikins, born in 1919, the librarian at Spellow Library, did much to motivate and organise poetry around the city. He had a desire to shock, never more so than when his wife committed suicide and he took up with, and later married, another poet, Sylvia Rice-Smith. The cover of their first book together, *A Black Look on the Bright Side* (1972), published by their own Toulouse Press, showed them in a graveyard. They appeared nude on the cover of the second one, *Harold and Sylvia Hikins's Book of Revelations* (1974).

Sidney Hoddes, a GP with a practice in Seaforth, wrote bittersweet poems of domestic life which may or may not have told you a lot about his wife, Cynthia, who was never seen at the readings. He wrote about sex and food and not much else, and he could be extremely funny ('My curry is going through a dangerous stage' from 'Menu', for example). I recall his wonderful joke about keeping man-sized Kleenex by the side of his bed, but there was desperation in his work that never fully surfaced. One of his poems, 'Promiscuity', was recorded by Scaffold but not released until 1998.

> Promiscuity, promiscuity,
> 'Tisn't a sin or vice,
> I don't really know if it's good for me,
> I just do it because it's nice.

Peggy Poole, another older poet, ran the well-attended 'Jabberwocky' evenings in the Wirral. I recall one poem about a lesbian relationship in South Africa years earlier. I assumed it was personal and I was stunned again by her candour in speaking so frankly. This was a long way from Pam Ayres.

I have fond memories of guest poets coming to Liverpool. Adrian Mitchell was always thought-provoking and I loved Christopher Logue's beautifully spoken dirty poems. Pete Brown impressed me at the Bluecoat Chambers; he read his new poems, which he said were really song lyrics and had just been recorded by Cream. Another strange brew.

Brian Jacques, who sang (and fought) with his brothers in the Liverpool Fishermen, wrote witty epic poems about historical events transposed to Liverpool. The problems of David and Goliath related to grazing rights in Sefton Park. Jakesy became a best-selling children's author and his presentation of classical music on BBC Radio Merseyside was so distinctive that he should have had a national programme. Also around was the schoolteacher Willy Russell, performing his songs on his own or with the Carlton Three. Rather than follow up the successes of *Educating Rita* and *Blood Brothers*, he has been appearing on poetry tours with Adrian, Roger and Brian.

I loved Roger McGough's poems and he could play with words brilliantly ('Hash Wednesday', 'What a shocking estate we are in', 'He aimed low in life and missed'). Many of his amusing poems packed a punch, but his deadly serious poem about Northern Ireland, 'A Brown Paper Carrier Bag' is among his best. McGough's wit and bite rival John Lennon's; he was as inventive a wordsmith and far more prolific, and he did, after all, write some of John's one-liners for *Yellow Submarine*. It is the funny poems I remember best, and his line, 'Who was the naughty girl who put Evostik in my contact lenses?' always runs through me.

Roger had contact lenses, standard glasses and prescription sunglasses and what he wore suited the occasion, but there was no side to him. I met him upstairs on a Ribble bus the week that 'Lily the Pink' was number one, and he seemed to think that there was nothing unusual in that. Judging by his collection, *Gig*, he never got sucked into the trappings of fame:

> I remember the days we stayed
> at the Albany. Five ten a night.
> I was somebody then (the one on the right
> With glasses singing 'Lily the Pink').
> The Dolce Vita.

The general public didn't know what to make of the poetry-with-music group Scaffold, and when they had their hits they played to the wrong audiences on variety shows. The cheerfully anarchic 'Summer with the Monarch' was a favourite in Liverpool, and yet recently McGough was in the frame for Poet Laureate. Ironically, Roger's poem 'If I were Poet Laureate' recommends Ken Dodd for Chancellor of the Exchequer.

I don't often pick up the books on my poetry shelf, so I'm glad to have had this opportunity. What has struck me is how many of the poems stand up today. They reflect a pride in the city (of course), a love of friendship, many remembrances of childhood, an intricate knowledge of public transport (few of the poets had cars) and a passion for a pint (with surprisingly few references to drugs). These books have a long shelf-life and I won't be putting them in a car boot sale for many years to come.

The Windows Project

Dave Ward

Why 'Windows'?

Back in 1974 a group of local residents on the Halewood estate were looking for a name for a poetry and music show that they were putting on in Bridgefield Sports Forum. 'Windows' was the title of a poem in the show by Icilda McLean who worked as a play leader and school meals assistant. It was adopted as the title of the production, which went down so well that 'Windows' became the title for regular poetry and music events staged every month in Halewood Library. These hosted visits by some of the leading poets of the day: Adrian Mitchell, Brian Patten, Fleur Adcock, Norman Nicholson, Libby Houston, Tom Pickard and many more combined with a committed nucleus of 'floor performers'. What had started as a one-off ran for ten years.

The events spawned two publications: *Arthur's Colour Supplement*, an offshoot of the *Halewood News* published by Halewood Community Council and delivering a mix of Halewood poetry, stories and pictures to every household on the Liverpool overspill housing estate; and *Smoke* magazine, from the outset combining contributions from leading poets such as Barry McSweeney, Miroslav Holub and Frances Horovitz with local and emerging talent and attracting artists with an eye for lively graphics.

Why 'Windows'?

In the summer of 1976 an invitation came from Merseyside Play Action Council for four poets to run writing workshops at Liverpool summer play schemes. Dave Calder and I had already combined to run a series of poetry performance events at Great Georges Community Cultural Project, where we had also learnt the value of introducing participation in the arts through specially devised games. We were joined by Carol Ann Duffy, just completing her degree at Liverpool University, and Libby Houston, already widely respected on the readings circuit. To help the youngsters to write in the high energy atmosphere of the play scheme at the Bronte Centre, situated next to the city centre Bullring housing, we created the Amazing Push Poem Machine (so named by Carol Ann) – a brightly coloured 12-foot ramp – up which the kids bowled a yellow football which dropped into a series of labelled crates, one for each letter of the alphabet.

The poems evolved one word at a time, each word starting with the letter the player had 'won' on the game. Poster-sized, zen-like surreal statements were created to be projected onto the walls of the end-of-week junior disco.

Why 'Windows'?

Following that first success Dave Calder and I were invited to take the workshops into more and more play schemes, devising a repertoire of non-competitive games – card games, board games and small-scale fairground style side-shows to encourage the children to write. It became a standing joke that whenever we asked for the use of a quieter space to help the kids to think, we would be ushered into a room that had no natural daylight.

In 1977–78, with the advent of Arts Council's community arts funding and Merseyside's Community Arts Assembly, came the opportunity to combine the Halewood-based performances and publications with the play scheme workshops and to create an independent organisation, which we named 'The Windows Project'.

Matt Simpson, then lecturer at Liverpool Institute of Higher Education, had been part of the original Halewood group and had suggested 'Windows' as the name. He became chair of the project's trustees when we obtained charitable status, but delighted even more in participating in summer play schemes – sharing the exhilaration of riding through the back streets of Liverpool on a flatback trailer carrying workshop equipment which included a four-foot-high model of a tower block and a huge sign reading 'City of Poems'.

During each of the week-long 'City of Poems' workshops the children constructed a model city with poems displayed on walls, traffic signs, advertising hoardings, rooftops and roads, replacing the language of advertising and signage. The 'City of Poems' became a metaphor for the development of Windows' work – the idea that poetry could become part of everyone's everyday life. To pursue that idea we continued to introduce writing workshops in a wide range of situations – from inner city to the outer limits.

During the following years, while continuing to expand the play scheme workshops, Windows received invitations from youth clubs, libraries and schools and began work with adults in sessions varying from day centres and care centres to writers' workshops (for those whose interest had already been stimulated), and library-based surgeries at the 'poetry advice desk'. Indeed Glyn Wright, whose subsequent first collection gathered numerous awards and who now regularly runs sessions for Windows, first made himself known to the Project via an enquiry at the advice desk.

While funding allowed, teams of poets were able to create multimedia works in collaboration with other artists. The top floor of Tower Hill Community Centre, Kirkby, was transformed into a space capsule incorporating sound effects, slide projections and installations by Radio Doom. The boxing gym in the same centre became the site for a large mural – a spectrum of colour poems within a 'window' frame.

In the confines of the corner of a crowded discotheque in Skelmersdale, communal poems were created before the writers sallied forth to combine with travelling circus workshops around the rural lanes of West Lancashire. Back in Liverpool, the Phantastic Phonetic Phactory culminated in a maze of latex and polystyrene words created with sculptor Peter Hatton, accompanied by a sound-scape of texts and body sounds made by David Collancz.

Further dimensions in sound and performance came when rap poets/jazz griots Levi Tafari and Muhammad Khalil (Eugene Lange) undertook some of their early workshops via the Project, later combining again with the Royal Liverpool Philharmonic Choir for a production based on poems from Knowsley schools staged at Liverpool's Everyman Theatre. More recently, Joan Owusu has brought her expertise of storytelling from many cultures and Jalal Nuriddin, founder of New York's Last Poets and architect of rap, has led workshops for young people.

At a series of city centre cafes, customers were surprised to find their tables laid with white linen cloths covered with handwritten lines of poetry. There were poems on the placemats and wall-hangings too, all presented in thematic black and white, including chequered table inlays with moveable black and white blocks. While they were sitting down to their mid-morning coffee, the customers were approached by waiters, also dressed in black and white, who offered them a selection from the 'poetry menu' – anything from an appetising word puzzle, to help with constructing a poem of their own, to table-side readings selected from a 'sweet trolley' of anthologies on a variety of themes.

Taking the techniques of involvement from the play scheme sessions, the 'menu' event, in collaboration with the Walker Art Gallery, presented poetry as participatory art to lunchtime cafe-goers. The metaphor of the City of Poems continued with 'Poetstreets', which moved into the landscape of actual streets with blow-ups of poems attached to street names that apparently commemorated 83 contemporary poets – though in reality they were more probably named after councillors who shared the same name! Windows also produced the country's longest-running Dial-a-Poem service, which provided a mixture of poetry, reviews and information and attracted 14,000 callers during its first year; it also published the successful Merseyside Poetry Minibook series, presenting new and established Merseyside poets in a standard pocket book format.

Today Windows involves the full range of writing – not only poets but also novelists, playwrights and storytellers who come together on a regular basis for their own skill-sharing sessions in the Project's new premises above News From Nowhere's bookshop at the heart of the Ropewalks quarter on Liverpool's busy Bold Street. This combines an administrative base and storage resource of workshop games and materials with library facilities featuring a unique collection of small press poetry publications dating back to the 1960s.

Workshop sessions now number between 500 and 700 every year, including some 150 through the Writers in Schools and Education Scheme (WISE), which the project administers on behalf of North West Arts Board. The Writers' Attachment Scheme is another recent development, extending the Project's own good practice of creating opportunities for new writers to become involved in workshops alongside established practitioners. The attachment scheme arranges pairings of mentors and trainees in three monitored settings – a school, a community venue and with disabled people.

Dave Calder has written up the Project's proliferation of games with accompanying workshops and examples as the *Windows Workbook*, available as hard copy or on disk from the Project, and has created a website (www.windowsproject.demon.co.uk).

Windows' aim continues to be to introduce the craft and creativity of writing in a wide range of settings, using workshop techniques which demonstrate that writing can be both inspirational and fun. Windows regularly involves up to 40 Merseyside writers each year, and the work has extended beyond the Merseyside base to Nottingham, Lincolnshire, Belfast, Derry, Leeds, Milton Keynes, the Isle of Man and Singapore.

Why 'Windows'?

Why not?

BROADER VIEWS

5

These Boys
The Rise of Mersey Beat

Richard Stakes

Introduction

The question of Merseyside's importance in the history of the development of pop music in the UK in the 1960s has been pondered many times. Why did such unprecedented developments occur in Liverpool and the surrounding areas, rather than in Southampton or Sheffield? Although other areas of the country had their own beat groups, some of which eventually came to national prominence, those from Merseyside were the ground-breakers. However, groups such as the Beatles, the Searchers and Gerry and the Pacemakers did not suddenly emerge 'out of nowhere'. Rather, Mersey Beat, as with many popular culture explosions, occurred in a period of experimentation and development, in its case dating back to earlier developments in pop music and the beginnings of rock'n'roll in Britain in the mid-1950s.

This chapter will analyse some of the socioeconomic and cultural factors that need to be taken into account when considering the origins of the Merseyside groups. It will argue that these influences were not just localised around the grey waters of the River Mersey, but were effecting change, particularly on youngsters, throughout the length and breadth of the country. Factors that will be considered include the changes in social life in post-war Britain and the 'US effect', as well as circumstances that can be identified within the Merseyside conurbation.

There's a Place

Merseyside is an amalgamation of a number of towns and cities surrounding the Mersey estuary on the west coast of England. The region was, until the boundary changes of 1974, set partially in Lancashire and partially in Cheshire, with the largest areas being Liverpool and Birkenhead on opposite banks of the river. According to the 1961 census, Liverpool was a city of some three-quarters of a million people. Liverpool was the second most important seaport in Britain after London, with connections to all parts of the world, but dealing particularly – in both human and commercial cargo – with the US.

Liverpool was a key place of embarkation for Eastern European immigrants who, having left their homeland, were travelling to a new life in the US. This was not just one-way traffic; Liverpool had, since the middle of the nineteenth century, been a port of embarkation for Irish immigrants wanting to travel in the same direction. Because some of these people lacked the funding to take them any further, Liverpool became their final destination. As with many other seaports, the city developed a cosmopolitan atmosphere encompassing the West Indian community in Toxteth, the Greek community, Chinatown and the Irish influence, which provided it with a distinct identity.

In the post-Second World War period, Liverpool was in slow decline. Changes in global political and economic circumstances meant that its main function as a port and shipbuilding centre was gradually disappearing. Liverpool in the early 1960s was becoming increasingly grim. Other areas of the country were outflanking a port that had been at its height during Victorian times. The demand for labour was at rock bottom; the city's buildings were the only reminders of its previous greatness. The bombing sustained in the Second World War hadn't helped either. In his unauthorised biography of Ringo Starr, Alan Clayson describes the district of Dingle, where the young Richard Starkey had grown up, in largely negative terms. It was, he wrote,

> One of the seediest districts of the blacked city... (with) rubbish sogging behind railings, outside lavatories... and corner shop windows barricaded with wire mesh... naked light bulbs covered in dust, damp plaster crumbled from the touch from cold walls... and noisy copper geysers hung above sinks in which a wife would both bathe babies and wash up dishes from a Sunday lunch on a newspaper tablecloth.[1]

Writing in the late 1960s, Nick Cohn was unimpressed. He described Liverpool as a 'strange town'. To him it was a place of 'real violence'.[2] This last point is described vividly by Gerry Marsden in his autobiography. About Dingle, where he also was brought up, he said: 'Dingle was no place for strangers and even if you lived there you kept strictly to your own area. There were dozens of gangs and you learned to take care of yourself'.[3] Marsden also describes the conscious territorialism of the bands, describing how they would play in venue in which they were unwelcome, and how fights would occur as a result. He says:

> I got smacked about a few times; the lads in the band had a few knuckles gone, loose teeth, black eyes, the occasional kick in the privates if they were unlucky. But there were no legs broken; it was simply a question of guarding your patch...[4]

Barry Miles similarly describes the experiences of McCartney and Harrison. McCartney described the violence between gangs in Speke, where he and Harrison lived, and the neighbouring area of Garston as akin to a 'frontier town in the wild west'.[5] It was, he says, 'very real... serious fighting'. Cohn, perhaps not surprisingly, feels that Liverpool, like many US cities, was a place of factions and gangs. He saw it as having an identity and style of its own and a private strength and humour, and as a city that is obsessed by everything it does. This humour had already produced nationally known figures such as Arthur Askey and Ted Ray. It was also to provide a vital ingredient to both the image and lyrics of pop musicians of the area. The Beatles for example became associated with sharp phrases and idiosyncratic humour that was capitalised on in their two early films *A Hard Day's Night* (1964) and *Help!* (1965). The humour of the area was also clearly exemplified by 'Thank You Very Much' (1967) and 'Lily the Pink' (1968) by local group Scaffold.

The obsessiveness described by Cohn was reported by George Melly, writing as another local made good, as 'patriotism'.[6] In his view it was essentially about Merseyside supporting its own. In this context, Gerry Marsden comments on the support he received from Liverpudlians just for living there after he and his group had become famous. Melly makes the same point about the local attitude towards the Beatles themselves. This continued as long as they stayed in Liverpool.

Liverpool, in geographical terms, faces towards America, and in commercial terms relationships were particularly strong with the countries across the Atlantic Ocean. This significance should not be overlooked in other areas either. To some extent, Merseyside faced the US in social and cultural terms also, and some of its characteristics were interchangeable with those of cities across the Atlantic. To Cohn, Liverpool was 'America in England'.[7] In the post-war world, he argues, this was case both musically and culturally.

The influence of the USA is well documented by both critics and members of the beat groups themselves.[8] This influence was largely brought about by the nature of Liverpool as a major seaport. Sailors returning from the USA with rhythm and blues records had an important impact on the local music scene. McCartney, for example, describes the draw of US music and its 'pull' on his ability to fully concentrate on his schoolwork.[9] Many of the records that found their way to Liverpool and influenced local performers were not seen as having the commercial potential to be released throughout Britain. Thus when some of these songs emerged on the first couple of Beatles LPs they were largely new to the rest of the country. Miles regards this as a great advantage to the Merseyside groups, providing them with a good source of material to support the self-penned material of Lennon and McCartney.

Those Were the Days

In a weary post-war Britain, the USA was regarded as having a degree of glamour. This was demonstrated particularly by the influence of the artefacts of American culture, such as colour comic books, as well as Hollywood films and the popular music of the period. The post-war British film industry was eventually swamped by American imports, as were the music charts after their introduction in Britain in 1952. Even before the inception of rock'n'roll in the mid-1950s, US artists such as Guy Mitchell, Doris Day, Frankie Laine and Johnnie Ray dominated the charts. American artists such as Bill Haley, the Everly Brothers and particularly Elvis Presley also dominated the rock'n'roll era.

Part of the glamour of the USA was its inaccessibility to most Britons. Mass inter-continental travel was still in its infancy in the mid-1960s. Similarly, American music was inaccessible, particularly the work of black rhythm and blues artists for whom there was little commercial market in Britain. There was often a delay in the release of US singles and albums; singles by even the most popular artists had often been at the top of the US charts before their release date here, adding to the glamour and excitement.

The American artists were not only regarded as glamorous; to many youngsters they also claimed authenticity, adding a heightened excitement that their British counterparts could not match. The main British rock'n'rollers – Tommy Steele, Terry Deene and Cliff Richard – were mainly pale copies of their American contemporaries. Indeed Steele's only number one hit 'Singing the Blues' was a cover of a US original by

Guy Mitchell. In order to appear on the TV programme *Oh Boy*, Cliff cut his sideburns and generally toned down his imitation of Elvis Presley on the orders of Jack Good, the show's producer. In this sense the American artists looked as if they were 'real'; those from the UK looked as if they wished they were. Unlike the majority of their American counterparts, many of Britain's rock'n'rollers underwent a professional change of name in order to heighten their glamour. Many of these pseudonyms were meant to highlight charisma and appeal. In this way Tommy Hicks became Tommy Steele, Harry Webb changed into Cliff Richard and Ronald Wycherley transmogrified into Billy Fury.

Billy Fury was an interesting precedent for events on Merseyside in the 1960s. A deck-hand on the Mersey tugboats by day, he had ambitions to become a songwriter. When Larry Parnes's 'Rock Extraveganza' package tour visited Birkenhead in 1958, he got backstage to talk to Marty Wilde, one of the headliners on the show. Wilde and his manager Parnes were impressed enough to sign him up and re-christen him in the now-traditional manner. However, in the style of later groups from the area, some of Fury's early hits were self-penned numbers.

Changes

Merseyside may have lacked the glamour of the USA as depicted in film or pop music, but nevertheless it was part of a country that was changing quickly in the late 1950s. It was a country of free compulsory education, full employment and growing social and economic expectations. In 1958, Prime Minister Harold Macmillan famously remarked that people 'had never had it so good'. By the end of the decade the first postwar generation had been through compulsory education up to the age of 15. Whatever they had made of it, it had given them a start in life denied to any previous generation; the world was their oyster. Social and geographical mobility was greater than ever before. For this generation the world was largely unexplored, and there were no real rules; social conventions were made to be broken, social class boundaries loosened and rules were invented as you went along.

Miles argues that the open entry system of art colleges and the end of National Service played particularly important parts in the changes that swept youth culture in the 1960s. At the time, any school leaver was able to attend art college provided that they could persuade the college to take them on. This resulted in these colleges becoming a hotbed for youngsters from very different social backgrounds and their ideas, eventually resulting in the promotion of British fashion in clothes, make-up and music, as well as art, both in Britain and throughout the rest of the world.

National Service had been a part of British life since the end of the Second World War. This two-year period of compulsory military training was finally abandoned in 1960. For Paul McCartney, this change was instrumental in the Beatles success for two reasons. First, it kept the Beatles together as a group at a time when, because of the differences in their ages, they would otherwise have been split up to do their service at different times. Secondly, he suggests that it also helped them to retain a freshness and a freedom that had been denied those only a few years older. He cites the case of Elvis Presley in particular:

> I always thought it ruined Elvis. We liked Elvis as a trucker, as a guy in jeans with swivelling hips, but didn't like him with the short haircut in the army calling everyone 'sir'. It just seemed he'd gone establishment, and his records after that weren't so good.[10]

Moreover, after the Depression of the 1930s and the austerity of the immediate post-war world of the late 1940s, Britain was entering an age of choice. This affected all generations, but for the young in particular it related to job opportunities, clothing and increased sexual freedom, particularly for teenagers.

Such changes can be particularly identified in some of the literature of the time. Examples of the genre include, most notably, Stan Barstow's A *Kind of Loving* (1960), a novel essentially about social conventions and respectability set in the West Riding of Yorkshire; E. R. Braithwaite's *To Sir With Love* (1959), about the trials and tribulations of teaching in a working-class school in the East End of London; and Alan Sillitoe's stark novel *Saturday Night and Sunday Morning* (1958), a study of growing up in Nottingham in the late 1950s.

The younger generation depicted in these novels and plays had been born and brought up in the post-war world as the first generation that did not move directly from childhood to adulthood; rather, they passed through the 'teenage'. This was not a biological change so much as an economic one; it had been conceived in the USA, where young people with money in their pockets were encouraged to spend their cash on items such as clothing and leisure activities.

The first representatives of this phenomenon were the 'teddy boys' of the mid-1950s. They were largely male and instantly recognisable by their clothing and hairstyles. Their clothes were a throwback to Edwardian days; long drapes and jackets with fur collars, accompanied by more modern trends in luminous socks and 'winkle-picker' shoes. Their hairstyles paid homage to Elvis: long on top, greasy and swept back from the forehead, with sideburns and a 'duck's arse' (DA) over the collar. It was the outward and largely superficial manifestation of teenage rebellion. From this perspective, the revolutionary appearance of rock'n'roll teenagers in the 1950s had become 'style' by the 1960s.

This fashion had an immense effect on the older generation, which was horrified not only by the look but also by the behaviour. The 1957 tour of Britain by Bill Haley saw the first outbreak of fan mania. He was mobbed on arrival at Waterloo Station in London, and his nationwide tour provoked unprecedented scenes of the stage being invaded and seats being ripped up by fans in the audience. This was the start of overt adolescent discontent and teenage rebellion. Teenagers were increasingly seen as part of a group that was separate, rebellious, different, striving to find something that was 'with it' and 'cool'.

Another major influence in Britain was the skiffle movement. This essentially 'home-grown' style, largely introduced and led by Lonnie Donegan from 1952 onwards, became a major movement towards the end of the decade. Skiffle, a largely 'do-it-yourself' movement, was inexpensive for the participants. For working-class kids with little money but great motivation, skiffle was often the starting point for the careers that followed – a spawning ground for the Merseyside kids, playing cheap guitars or drums and often encouraged by their parents, who were later to become trend-setters.

Liverpool Oratorio

The influence of rock'n'roll stars such as Bill Haley, Elvis Presley and Little Richard had a great impact on pop music. Throughout the late 1950s and early 1960s, pop music increasingly became a vehicle for leisure activities for the young as well as a conduit for their emotions. The former was certainly the case on Merseyside which, from late 1950s onwards, crawled with 'beat groups' usually composed of three guitarists and a drummer. The actual number of such groups in the area is not known; John Peel has spoken of 250, Nick Cohn's estimate was upwards of 350, and Gerry Marsden describes 'literally hundreds of groups'.[11] This was not just a Merseyside phenomenon; it was the case up and down the country.

The evidence from local literature suggests that the difference around Liverpool lay in the style of music played. Whereas in many areas of the country Cliff Richard's backing group the Shadows were the key influence, Merseysiders were far more influenced by American rhythm and blues artists. A number of artists detail how they went to Brian Epstein's record shop to order records by largely unknown artists that were difficult to obtain in the UK.

A particularly striking example of the influence of US rhythm and blues can be seen in the Beatles' first LP *Please Please Me*, released in 1963. This LP comprises 14 tracks: eight Lennon and McCartney songs, and six others that were live favourites, including five that clearly demonstrated rhythm and blues influences: 'Baby It's You' and 'Boys', originally performed by the Shirelles; 'Anna', written by Arthur Alexander, an Afro-American from Alabama; 'Chains', a Jerry Goffin and Carole King song that had been a minor hit for the Dimensions in the USA; and 'Twist and Shout', a cover of a 1962 US hit by the Isley Brothers. Despite this Tony Barrow, the writer of the sleeve notes, largely dismisses the assertion. Barrow's notes, while paying respect to the rhythm and blues tradition of black America, assert that the Merseyside beat groups reinterpreted these songs to produce 'the unique brand of Rhythm and Blues on Merseyside... which the Beatles themselves have helped to pioneer since their formation in 1960'. It is undoubtedly the case, as autobiographical interviews have shown, that US rhythm and blues had a great degree of influence on many Merseyside groups. This, along with a sound that was distinctive to the instrumentation and the vocal delivery of white English bands, gave the Mersey groups a certain uniqueness.

Let 'em in

In his study of the social history of rock'n'roll, Pete Freidlander argued that each fashion in pop music has a life cycle of three phases.[12] These phases he describes as formulation, maturation and normalisation. Formulation occurs while the style acquires its form and shape, borrowing from sources to survive and grow. Maturation is reached when the artists experiment with ways to improve and enhance the form, while normalisation occurs when the style is either unable or unwilling to evolve further and begins to stagnate, become out of touch, and caricature or even parody itself.

It is also Freidlander's view that a popular music life cycle will last, at most, between seven and ten years. His evidence is drawn from the US tradition but this can be seen in the British context as well. The Mersey Beat boom occurred in Britain in 1963, some eight years after the start of rock'n'roll. Hard rock appeared at the end of the 1960s and punk, perhaps the natural successor to the music of the sixties generation, was beginning to make its first impressions some ten years later. This is a time-scale that spans a single generation of adolescents, taking them from pre-pubescence to late teenager, and from the age of naivety to adulthood.

Freidlander's thesis has other points to recommend it. The UK charts of 1962 displayed a number of examples of what can be best described as stagnation. Apart from the obvious chart toppers from Elvis and Cliff, none of which could be classified as rock'n'roll records, other hits included such 'rock'n'rollers' as Frank Ifield, Mike Sarne (an example of rock parody if there ever was one) and instrumentals by Acker Bilk, B. Bumble, the Shadows and the Tornados. The year's best-sellers list included caricatures of rock'n'roll by Elvis Presley ('Rock-a Hula Baby') and Karl Denver ('Wimoweh'). In such circumstances it is hardly surprising that a fillip was called for, and Mersey Beat fitted the bill admirably. The music was refreshing and full of vitality. The group members were young, fresh-faced, energetic and had an authenticity that was novel to British pop music at that time. It was hardly surprising that it swept across the charts. Perhaps surprisingly it was Gerry and the Pacemakers who hit the number one spot first in April. Gerry's status was surprising in that the Mersey sirens had been sounded initially by the Beatles. By spring 1963 the Beatles had had two hits: 'Love Me Do' (number 17 in December 1962) and 'Please Please Me' (surprisingly only reaching number 2 in January and February 1963, behind the seemingly ubiquitous Frank Ifield).

However, once the dam was breached the beat groups flooded in. Gerry and the Pacemakers were followed by the Beatles again in May (with 'From Me to You') while Gerry took over top spot again in July. After a brief three-week respite in late July Merseyside was back again in August. And how! With a brief interval in October, allowing East Anglia's answer to Merseyside, Brian Poole and the Tremeloes, to take over the top spot, the Mersey groups dominated the top of the hit parade for the rest of the year. The groups included the Searchers ('Sweets for my Sweet') and Billy J. Kramer and the Dakotas ('Bad to Him') as well as Gerry and the Pacemakers with the song that was to become an anthem for the red side of Liverpool, 'You'll Never Walk Alone', and the Beatles on three separate occasions ('She Loves You', which originally hit the top of the table in September for four weeks only to return again for a couple of weeks in November, and 'I Want to Hold your Hand', which was at the top for five weeks around Christmas).

Perhaps of even greater significance than the assault on the singles chart was that on the albums list. In 1963 the Beatles had two number ones in the LP chart, *Please Please Me* and *With the Beatles*. The Searchers also had two top ten albums in 1963 (*Meet the Searchers* and *Sugar and Spice*). Gerry and the Pacemakers reached number two with an album perhaps appropriately called *How Do You Like It?* while Billy J. Kramer and the Dakotas made the top 20 with *Listen to Billy J Kramer*.

The significance of this lies in the contrast between the style of these groups and the records that usually topped this chart. The *Guinness Book of Hit Albums*[13] records that, from its inception in 1958 until 1963, this chart was dominated by non-rock albums such as *West Side Story*, *The Sound of Music* and *The Black and White Minstrel Show*. It was a domination that was to be irreparably broken, as illustrated by an examination of the period between 1963 and 1968, when only one non-rock album hit the top of the charts. In the circumstances it is perhaps not surprising that the seventh edition of *The Guinness Book of Hit Albums* describes the circumstances as 'a musical revolution'.

In many ways the charts of 1964 were not dissimilar to those of the previous year. Their domination by Mersey Beat was not as strong, but the Beatles, the Searchers and Billy J. Kramer all had number one hit singles, as they had had the previous year. They were joined at the top by a new Merseyside face, Cilla Black, who had her only chart topper that year. The album chart also had a similar look to that of 1963. The Beatles had two more chart toppers and the Searchers two more top ten entries. However, both Gerry and the Pacemakers and Billy J. Kramer failed to score in the album chart. Gerry, so far, has returned only once more (in 1965) and Billy has never repeated his first success.

By 1965 it was largely over for most of the Mersey groups. Some went into the cabaret circuit; others returned to Liverpool, after their 15 minutes of fame, while Cilla Black eventually became a national television personality. Of course the Beatles went on from strength to strength, conquering the USA and the rest of the world and, along with other 1960s luminaries such as Bob Dylan, changing the face of pop music forever. However, as they say, that is another story!

Notes

1 Alan Clayson, *Ringo Starr, Straight Man or Joker?*, London, Sidgwick and Jackson, 1991, p. 2.

2 Nick Cohn, *WopBopaLopBopLopBamBoom*, London, Paladin, 1969, pp. 147–8.

3 Gerry Marsden with R. Coleman, *I'll Never Walk Alone: An Autobiography*, London, Bloomsbury, 1993, p. 9.

4 Marsden, *I'll Never Walk Alone*, p. 31.

5 Barry Miles, *Paul McCartney, Many Years From Now*, London, Secker and Warburg, 1997, pp. 11–13.

6 George Melly, *Revolt into Style: The Pop Arts in Britain*, London, Penguin, 1970, p. 71.

7 Cohn, *WopBopaLopBopLopBamBoom*, p. 148.

8 Cohn, *WopBopaLopBopLopBamBoom*; Melly, *Revolt into Style*; I. MacDonald, *Revolution in the Head: The Beatles' Records and the Sixties*, London, Fourth Estate, 1994; A. Clayson, *The Quiet One: A Life of George Harrison*, London, Sidgwick and Jackson, 1990; Clayson, *Ringo Starr*; Marsden, *I'll Never Walk Alone*; Miles, *Paul McCartney*.

9 Miles, *Paul McCartney*.

10 Miles, *Paul McCartney*, p. 55.

11 Marsden, *I'll Never Walk Alone*, p. 12.

12 Pete Friedlander, *A Social History of Rock'n'Roll*, Boulder, CO, Westview, 1996.

13 P. Gambaccini, T. Rice and J. Rice, *The Guinness Book of Hit Albums*, Enfield, Guinness Publishing, 7th edn, 1996.

Jazz Scene, Liverpool Scene

The Early 1960s

Pete Townsend

that's jazz you hear in the salt cellars
but they don't let non-members in...
Roger McGough, *Summer with Monika*

Although the jazz world was unaware of the fact, by the early 1960s its last period of cultural ascendancy was coming to an end. Within a few years, and especially after the stunning impact of the Beatles on the USA in 1964, rock would begin to take the place of jazz in all the culturally prestigious areas in which jazz had seemed to be the most expressive and important modern popular musical form. Jazz was still heard up to the mid-1960s, for instance, in film music, but rock would soon take over this function, as it would a few years later take over the job of being the most creative, even avant-garde and experimental musical form, suitable for expressing the radical political and artistic notions that swarmed around the upheavals of the late 1960s.

For jazz musicians, the Beatles and everything that followed them were an economic disaster. The bottom fell out of the jazz business within a very short time, and the slump lasted until well into the 1980s. The established US stars carried on unaffected by this, but the most dramatic change for the average jobbing jazz player was the loss of the prospect of steady work in clubs and bars, and employment in bands providing music for TV and radio, advertising jingles, stage shows and the like, as the public preference changed once and for all towards a rock-flavoured music.

But jazz left its trace, even on the music, art and poetry of the late 1960s that seemed in some ways to be its antithesis. The cultural scene that followed jazz would not have been as it was without the presence of jazz just a few years earlier. Some of the artists concerned, notably Adrian Henri, acknowledge the direct influence of jazz on their work;

but the more pervasive influence of jazz is found in the general mindset that the jazz scene had created when it was alive, visible and important.

Jazz had different identities in its international, national and local (in this case Liverpudlian) settings. At all three of these levels, however, the picture changed in a similar way between 1960 and 1965. In 1960 there was a viable and coherent jazz economy; by 1965, at all three levels, it was starting to disappear rapidly. The worldwide impact of the beat scene that Liverpool spawned had its effect right through the world of music, from the recording policies of major US music corporations, to band musicians working for the BBC, to one-night-a-week trombonists in pubs on the Wirral.

Jazz had already been through some difficult times even before it was knocked down by the rock juggernaut in 1964. In retrospect it seems that the classic signs of imminent decline should already have been detectable, as some forms of jazz lost interest in maintaining popular support and attempted self-consciously to produce more sophisticated and difficult music. Even the jazz of Charlie Parker, Dizzy Gillespie and Thelonious Monk in the 1940s had, through no fault of the musicians, become associated with intellectualism in a way that had never been the case with jazz before. In the 1950s this tendency tried to recast the cultural image of jazz into something that looked more like European classical music. Sometimes this classicising of jazz was superficial, involving the introduction of 'classical' instruments such as the oboe and the cello, but some jazz musicians of the time wanted to become composers in the European sense, as well as mere players of jazz. It was understood by sections of the jazz community that the music was about to take the next evolutionary step towards becoming a 'serious' form like European classical music – and that it might even blend with it.

What effectively put a stop to this was an opposing tendency among some jazz players to remember its African roots and to reclaim its identity as a black music. This started in the late 1950s with the 'funky' or 'soul' jazz of players such as Cannonball Adderley, and the conscious return to the simplicity of the blues in the various groups led by Charles Mingus. Over the next few years, this tendency rejected the popular song form, searched for distinctively African musical elements, and arrived, in the person of Ornette Coleman, at a radical 'free' jazz. Some of these innovations gave the music a temporary popular appeal, but some of the free playing of Coleman, and more especially of Albert Ayler and Cecil Taylor, was relatively audience-unfriendly. The music sometimes became attached to the radical black nationalist politics advocated by practitioners or by writers like LeRoi Jones.

So, by the early 1960s, jazz was attached to some fairly weighty issues. The air of intellectualism that modern jazz had been wearing since the 1940s was now complicated by the addition of political debates on the ownership of the music, on race, and by the idea that jazz, like 'serious' music, needed to progress, to experiment, to have an avant-garde. Jazz was no longer to be thought of as music for fun or entertainment, it had no truck with popular music and showbusiness; it was less interested in holding on to an audience than in following through its own progressive lines of development. When the Beatles turned up in the USA in 1964, jazz was ready to have the economic props kicked out from under it.

The situation on the British jazz scene was similar in some ways; British jazz players still got some of their sense of direction from following what was happening in the USA. In the 1950s British modern jazz, too, went through a classical phase, and this was then followed by a move towards free jazz in the early 1960s. Although this sounded quite similar to the music being created by people like Ornette Coleman and John Coltrane, free jazz in Britain came without the black militancy of some of the American players and of writers like LeRoi Jones, for the principal reason that very few of the British musicians were themselves black. British jazz had its 'modernists', working in the idioms of Charlie Parker and Miles Davis, and it had its avant-gardists, with groups such as the Spontaneous Music Ensemble purveying uncompromising atonal, collective, totally free improvisations.

What was peculiar to the British jazz scene as a whole, however, was the amazing persistence and popularity of a much older style of jazz deriving from the music of New Orleans in the 1920s. Although many British players in these styles had come to the music through listening to the originals, the main impulse for the resurgence of what was in principle an archaic way of playing jazz came from the 'revivalist' movement that began in the USA around 1940. The revivalist attitude could be purist, academic, even ideological – in some respects a reaction to the more commercial 'swing' styles of the 1930s and 1940s, it claimed to rediscover the 'true' jazz of the pioneers, the musicians who had nurtured the music in New Orleans when it was still a music of the people. Musicians in the various revivalist groups tended to return to the original instrumentation of a New Orleans band, with the front line of trumpet, trombone and clarinet backed by a rhythm section typically, almost symbolically, containing a banjo. Instruments identified with later jazz styles, such as the saxophone and the guitar, were out of favour.

The revivalist movement in its many forms never caught on in the USA in the way it did in Britain. The type of jazz that had its roots in New Orleans took on a life of its own in the UK, and maintained a large youth audience from the late 1940s right through to the immediate pre-Beatles period of 1962–63. It seemed to lock into a number of the significant cultural and political scenes of the period, from the political CND/Ban the Bomb axis to the cultural and artistic domain of the art schools and the beatniks. Traditional jazz, as it came to be called, was the background music to a lot of the intellectual, political and artistic activity of young Britons from the end of the war up to the Beatlemania years.

Traditional jazz in Britain, though it was associated with dancing, alcohol and all-night 'raves', still had an aspect of greater earnestness and intensity to it than did rock'n'roll, which was hedonistic in a more consumerist style. The musicians themselves tended to be historically aware and were sometimes reverential towards the sources of their music. Since New Orleans music was the self-expression of an oppressed black community, respect for the music tended to imply a freedom from racial prejudice, a sympathy with the marginalised that carried over into a more general political radicalism. Jazz in its sensuality and its identification with unrestrained behaviour was the most easily available form of revolt against the pervasively straightlaced 1950s Britain, and, until rock strengthened its hold over a young audience in the 1960s, was the nearest thing that Britain had to a youth subculture.

Traditional jazz, though deliberately backward-looking as a musical style, nevertheless provided, in the British context, an arena for creativity that was otherwise lacking. One of the conditions of musicianship in this field was that it was amateur, home-made, personal. Most players were self-taught, operating in happy ignorance of music schools and the canon of 'great music'. Some simply put together a technique that would just about carry them through the New Orleans repertoire that they heard on records or from other British players, but had no other musical pretensions. They realised that, in jazz, individuality counts for a great deal, and that individuality can be achieved in all kinds of backhanded ways.

One of the notable features of the British jazz-playing community of this era is the interpenetration of the arts. Many people who were jazz players, particularly in the traditional school, were also involved in other artistic activities: painting, cartoons, acting, writing. Many people known principally as writers or painters had a stint in a traditional jazz band, in the same way perhaps that Tony Blair, Bill Clinton and the men of their generation are known to have dabbled with rock.

One of these comminglings in particular has had a continuing, if occasional, relevance to the development of poetry – the jazz-and-poetry movement that flourished, if that's the word, during the late 1950s. One of the impulses for this, again, came from the US scene. Jazz with poetry, a kind of performance setting in which a jazz band accompanied a reciting poet, had been tried as long ago as the 1920s by writers such as Langston Hughes, but its most celebrated reappearance was among the San Francisco writers of the 1950s. The moving force seems to have been the poet Kenneth Rexroth, who organised public performances in San Francisco, and who, along with more famous colleagues such as Jack Kerouac, made numerous recordings of jazz with poetry during the period. Rexroth's own opinion, and that of many critics of both jazz and poetry, was that the two art forms impeded one another rather than blending. 'It was ruined', he said, 'by people who knew nothing about either jazz or poetry.'

History has taken a kinder view of the jazz-and-poetry movement, especially in recent years, when there seems to have been a reawakening of interest in its artistic possibilities: Adrian Henri, for example, has recently issued a recording in the jazz and poetry style. In the late 1950s and early 1960s, in any case, the impetus was continued in Britain by poets such as Christopher Logue and Pete Brown. In the hands of writers such as Brown and Henri, jazz-with-poetry mutated gradually into rock-with-poetry as, towards the mid-1960s, the musical style of the day was changing.

In 1961–62 the jazz boom reached its commercial pinnacle in the form of 'trad', a version of the New Orleans style that had been tarted up for commercial effect by having the musicians wear costumes and play lightly jazzed-up renditions of pop tunes. At this stage, most British towns still supported a network of jazz clubs where jazz in its various styles was still available; this network was dominated by the traditional jazz circuit that for a decade or more had sustained travelling bands like those described by George Melly in *Owning Up*.[1] Some bands toured the provinces, but most of their business was in the cities. Leeds, Manchester and Liverpool had extensive jazz scenes that remained relatively big business up until the post-Beatles crash. Manchester, for example, had a major venue for visiting US jazz stars, the Sports Guild, as well as its own local jazz stratum of pubs and clubs. The Liverpool jazz scene included regular jazz events at the Picton Hall, city centre clubs and pubs, and jazz activity spreading out into smaller-scale venues in the suburbs. It was in such places as these, by necessity, that the insurgent rock bands played some of their earliest gigs. Some of the Beatles' engagements, in the years before their major success, were in clubs that still were primarily dedicated to jazz, though the Beatles themselves were in the process of changing that. They played gigs at the Pavilion in New Brighton; there was a trad band on the same bill. They were the support band to the then king of British trad, Acker Bilk, in a 'riverboat shuffle' on the Mersey in the summer of 1961. At the Cavern club, now a place of pilgrimage for lovers of rock but then a staunchly jazz venue, the Beatles were instructed on their first gig to 'Cut out the bloody rock'.

Rock, however, took over. Like the rabbit holes on coastal islands that become birds' nests, the same venues that for years had been supporting a jazz economy turned into the infrastructure of the rock scene. Trad was killed off in quick time by the huge popularity of the Beatles, the Rolling Stones and those who followed them, and jazz retreated to the marginal position where it has remained for most of the subsequent 40 years. Even by the mid-1960s, jazz as a musical form and as a cultural influence had lost all the ground that it had occupied only a few years before. The movement of poets such as Brown and Henri towards rock reflected a sense that it, not jazz, was the most creative environment to be working in. Rock was bolstered by the shift that Bob Dylan took in the mid-1960s away from folk music towards a rock aesthetic, and by the growing creative self-consciousness of rock writers such as Lennon and McCartney.

The visible influence of jazz on the Liverpool poetry scene is limited in scope; it is more evident in Henri than in McGough, and less so in Brian Patten's work, which is generally less oriented towards music. One of the routes that this influence took was more indirect, via the American Beat writers. Jazz was not in fact as pervasive an influence on the Beats as it is sometimes reputed to be: it is often bundled together with their poetry, lifestyles, tastes in narcotics, clothes and experiences as elements of a historically vague myth of 'the 1950s'. In actuality, some of the Beats knew or cared little about jazz. The exception that confused the issue was Jack Kerouac, whose interest in jazz was serious and lifelong. Jazz also meant something, however, to both Allen Ginsberg and Gregory Corso, two of the most apparent Beat influences on the Liverpool writers. The Beat writers passed on to British poets this sense of a jazz-conditioned creative environment, or an environment in which various art forms, including jazz and poetry, somehow live together. This to some extent paralleled the British writers' experience of the jazz-drenched 1950s and early 1960s creative scene in this country.

Adrian Henri's mid-1960s poem 'Me', a list of artistic heroes, includes the names of eight jazz musicians among painters, writers, composers, radical political figures and all four members of the Beatles. Henri's eight jazz figures are indicative, as such lists are, of a personal perspective: four were important modernists (Parker, Adderley, Thelonious Monk and Miles Davis), one was a deeply poetic female blues singer (Bessie Smith), and the others were three of the players at the cutting edge of the radical 1960s avant-garde: Roland Kirk, Charles Mingus and John Coltrane, the last the towering figure of the period, representative of both restless artistic experimentation and black pride.

Charlie 'Bird' Parker turns up again as one of the imaginary witnesses to 'Adrian Henri's Last Will and Testament', disposing of, among other things, a collection of Charlie Mingus records. Mingus is also one of the dedicatees of the earlier poem 'Tonight at Noon'. References to jazz players such as Mingus, Miles Davis and another restless, exploratory improviser, Sonny Rollins, crop up irregularly throughout Henri's poetry. The section of *Autobiography* on the years 1957–64 recalls 'sharing with you/ Bird, Monk and Mingus'.

What is noticeable in the picture of jazz as it is manifested in Henri's poetry is how much it reflects the exceptional and the radical. Of the eight players mentioned so far, all represent some degree of transcendence: Parker, the primary inventor of bebop, a style that has been considered not only as musically but also politically radical in its immediate post-war context; Davis, the multiple re-inventor of jazz styles, leading the move towards modal harmony in the mid-1950s; Mingus, the rediscoverer of the earthy blues roots underneath the complexity of bebop; Coltrane, the most far-reaching and restless of all in his constant, almost obsessive examination of scales, modes, harmonies and African rhythms. These are artists and breakers of moulds, jazz musicians worthy to keep company with the likes of Blake, Pollock, Stravinsky and the rest of Henri's nominees.

There is little interest in what you might call 'normal' jazz, the kind of idiomatic music that provided the basic everyday language through the 1940s and 1950s. Henri picks out the disruptive artistic geniuses. There is even very little representation of the background British jazz world of pubs and clubs, apart from, for example, a stray reference in a later section of *Autobiography* to 'falling headfirst down a stone colonnade at a Jazz Band Ball'. Jazz seems to be of little interest as a social phenomenon in the form in which it was inevitably encountered on the musical scene of the 1950s and early 1960s.

A second distinguishing feature of Henri's jazz icons is that they are American. Jazz is so deeply American an art that this seems hardly worth pointing out, but jazz was only one of a number of cultural domains in which British writers looked towards the USA. Henri also cites American painters (Rothko, Pollock, Rauschenberg and Johns) and writers (Poe, Hemingway, Burroughs and Bradbury) among his pantheon of great names. Among these, the presence of Parker, Davis, Monk and Coltrane only confirms an impression that the USA represents the innovation, the rebellion, the intensity of experiment and self-expression that could only exist in a society unlike that of Britain in the first couple of decades after the war.

There is a sense of discovery and revelation in Henri's references to jazz: reminiscences of hearing the music for the first time, records of new artistic sensations, indications of the ways in which painting and poetry might move in the same directions. For British musicians from the 1930s through to the mid-1960s, jazz often provided this sense of the revelation of an new artistic universe beyond the familiar one. Jazz musicians such as George Melly and Humphrey Lyttleton have written about searching out the few rare jazz records that found their way through to Britain, chance encounters with the music that came from across the water from the different universe on the other side of the Atlantic. For Liverpool musicians of the Beatles generation, these encounters were with the rhythm and blues records brought back by the transatlantic ships. The generation that John Lennon and Paul McCartney belonged to had its ears opened by Jimmy Reed and Bo Diddley rather than Louis Armstrong and Charlie Parker.

The poetry of Adrian Henri and Roger McGough parallels this shift of taste and experience. They straddle the two generations that were just starting to change places by the early 1960s: the jazz generation, whose lives were marked by austerity, National Service, jazz and socialism, gave way to the rock generation, conditioned by relative prosperity, social mobility, and rock'n'roll. References to artists in the world of rock cluster just as strongly in Henri's poetry as the jazz musicians: Chuck Berry, Little Richard, and again and again, the Rolling Stones and the Beatles. By the late 1960s Henri and McGough, together with writers such as Pete Brown, were aligned with the world of rock music, or were operating on its fringes, Henri with the Liverpool Scene, Brown with the Battered Ornaments, and McGough with Scaffold, who appeared on *Top of the Pops*. The time of jazz as a focus of creative energy was over, and the signs of its end had been apparent for some time. It had been the soundtrack for the lives of many artists in many media. It had provided an example of individual creativity away from the influence of schools and canons of great art. It had been one route by which the democratising tendency of American popular artistic forms, including poetry, had found its way into the lives and works of British writers, painters and musicians.

Notes

1 George Melly, *Owning Up*, London, Weidenfeld & Nicolson, 1965.

Notes on Contributors

Carole Baldock is coordinator of the Dead Good Poets Society, which holds monthly Open Floors and guest evenings at the Pilgrim pub, Liverpool. She is also a well-known editor and writer on writing skills. Her many activities include being reviews editor for *Orbis* and running Cherrybite Publications. Author of several books, she is editorial director of www.poettext.com and editor of *Competition Bulletin*.

Peter Barry was born and brought up in Liverpool and attended London University (King's College and the Institute of United States Studies). He taught at LSU, Southampton, for several years before moving in 1995 to the University of Wales, Aberystwyth, where he is now reader in English. He has published 40 or so articles and is the author of *Beginning Theory* (1995) and *Contemporary British Poetry and the City*, both from Manchester University Press. He is poetry and reviews editor for *English* (the journal of the English Association).

David Bateman was born in Kent in 1957. He is a freelance writer and teaches poetry and creative writing part-time for the University of Liverpool, Liverpool City Council and the Windows Project. He is also researching and writing a history of poetry in Liverpool (to be published by Headland), and is editing anthologies of Liverpool poetry. He has performed his poetry at pubs, clubs, theatres and festivals throughout Britain. Poetry publications include *From Jellybeans to Reprobation* (Hybrid, 1996) and *Curse of the Killer Hedge* (Iron, 1996). Forthcoming is *The Sweetness of Nightingales.*

Spencer Leigh was born in 1945 and spent many memorable evenings listening to the Liverpool poets during the 1960s and early 1970s. He has a twice-weekly music show on BBC Radio Merseyside and has written several music books including *Memories of Buddy Holly* (with Jim

Dawson, Big Nickel Publications, 1996), *Halfway to Paradise: Britpop 1955–62* (Finbarr International, 1996), *Drummed Out! The Sacking of Pete Best* (Northdown Publishing, 1998), *Brother Can You Spare a Dime? 100 Years of Hit Songwriting* (Spencer Leigh Ltd, 2000) and *Baby, That is Rock and Roll: American Pop 1954–1963* (Finbarr International, 2001). He writes for several magazines as well as supplying obituaries of musical personalities for *The Independent*. He says, 'I was delighted when Andrew Motion praised Bob Dylan's "Visions of Johanna". I have always thought that the best rock lyrics are poetry.'

Michael Murphy's poems have appeared widely in journals including *Poetry Review*, *Poetry Ireland Review* and *London Magazine*. A first collection, *After Attila* (Shoestring Press, 1998) includes his translations of the Hungarian poet Attila József. In 2000 he was awarded a North West Arts Writer's Bursary, and he is shortlisted for the 2001 Dearmer Prize. He is the editor of *The Collected George Garrett* (Trent Editions, 1999) which brings together for the first time all of Merseyside-born Garrett's fiction and reportage. His essays on modern and contemporary poetry have appeared in the UK, Europe and Australia, and in 2000 he completed a doctoral thesis on poetry and exile.

Deryn Rees-Jones is Reader in Poetry at Liverpool Hope University College. She has written a monograph on Carol Ann Duffy in the British Council/Northcote House series, and is in the final stages of completing a book of essays on women's poetry in Britain since 1940, *Consorting with Angels*, for Bloodaxe. She is also the co-editor, with Alison Mark, of *Contemporary Women's Poetry: Reading/Writing/Practice* (Macmillan, 2000). *The Memory Tray* (1994) was shortlisted for a Forward Prize, and *Signs Round a Dead Body* (1998) was a PBS special recommendation.

Matt Simpson lives in Liverpool. He retired from lecturing at Liverpool Hope University College in 1998. He has published ten pamphlets of poetry and six full-length collections – three of these with Bloodaxe Books: *Making Arrangements* (1982), *An Elegy for the Galosherman* (1990) and *Catching Up with History* (1995). Since then he has published *Cutting the Clouds Towards* (Liverpool University Press), *Somewhere Down the Line* (Shoestring), both in 1998, and *Getting There* (Liverpool University Press, 2001). He has published two collections of poems for children, *The Pig's Thermal Underwear* (Headland, 1994) and *Lost Property Box* (Macmillan, 1995) as well as a number of reviews and essays. In 1995 he was poet-in-residence in Tasmania.

Richard Stakes is a lecturer in Education at Doncaster College and freelance writer specialising in the area of special needs. He is currently researching autism at Sheffield Hallam University. Main publications are (with Garry Hornsby) *Meeting Special Needs in Mainstream Schools* (David Fulton, 2nd edn, 2000) and *Change in Special Education* (Cassell, 1997). His familiarity with educational issues is surpassed by his encyclopaedic knowledge of 1960s pop music.

Levi Tafari was born and raised in Liverpool by his Jamaican parents. He attended the Liverpool 8 Writers Workshop to get the intellectual stimulation he needed, and he was soon part of the performance scene. His work has always been rooted in the oral tradition of the griot. Levi has teamed up with reggae, soul and funk fusion bands, and has been poet-in-residence with the Royal Liverpool Philharmonic Orchestra. He has published three collections of poetry and has made guest appearances on television. In 1997 a documentary was made about his journey to Ethiopia.

Pete Townsend is Senior Lecturer in English at the University of Huddersfield, and a freelance writer. His main interests are literature and jazz, and he has published a collection of poetry, *For Jazz* (published in the US), as Peter McSloy. His latest publication is *Jazz and American Culture* (Edinburgh University Press, 2000). He has also performed widely at literary festivals and on the poetry circuit. In 1999 he gave a lecture at the Duke Ellington Centenary Conference in Washington

Stephen Wade's latest publications include *Jewish American Literature since 1945* (Edinburgh University Press, 1999) and *Write Yourself a New Life* (How To Pathways, 2000). He is Senior Lecturer in English at the University of Huddersfield.

Dave Ward was born in Northampton. He was a member of Adrian Mitchell's Song Workshop at Lancaster University, where he took part in the first BA Creative Writing module under David Craig. Publications include *Candy and Jazzz* (OUP), *Jambo* (Impact), *Tracts* (Headland) and *The Tree of Dreams* (as David Graygoose, Harper Collins). His poetry has been widely broadcast and anthologised. Dave has been coordinator of the Windows Project since 1976.

Select Bibliography

Ambit no 158, special issue on Liverpool, London, 1999

Peter Aughton, *Liverpool: A People's History*, London, Carnegie Press, 1990

Martin Booth, *British Poetry 1964–1984*, London, Routledge & Kegan Paul, 1985

Phil Bowen, *A Gallery to Play To*, Exeter, Stride, 1999

Howard Channon, *Portrait of Liverpool*, London, Robert Hale, 1969

Linda Cookson, *Brian Patten*, Plymouth, Northcote House, 1997

John Cornelius, *Liverpool 8*, London, John Murray, 1982; reprinted Liverpool, Liverpool University Press, 2001

Adrian Henri, *Paintings 1953–1998*, Liverpool, NMGM, 1999

Grevel Lindop, 'Poetry, Rhetoric and the Mass Audience: The Case of the Liverpool Poets', in G. Lindop and M. Schmidt, *British Poetry since 1960*, Manchester, Carcanet, 1972

Edward Lucie-Smith, *The Liverpool Scene*, London, Donald Carroll, 1967

Peter Robinson (ed.), *Liverpool Accents*, Liverpool, Liverpool University Press, 1996

Index